Should We Ever Say, "I Am Saved"?

What it means to be assured of salvation

Herbert E. Douglass

Pacific Press® Publishing Association
Nampa, Idaho
Oshawa, Ontario, Canada
www.pacificpress.com

Cover design by Tim Larson
photo by Panoramic Images ©

Copyright © 2003 by
Pacific Press® Publishing Association
Printed in United States of America
All Rights Reserved

Additional copies of this book may be purchased at
http://www.adventistbookcenter.com

Unless otherwise indicated, Scripture quotations are taken from the
New King James Version, Copyright © 1979, 1980, 1982, Thomas
Nelson, Inc., Publishers.

Library of Congress Cataloging-in-Publication Data

Douglass, Herbert E.
Should We Ever Say "I Am Saved?" What it means to be
assured of Salvation/ Herbert E. Douglass.
p. cm.
Includes bibliographical references
ISBN: 0-8163-1967-7
1. Assurance (Theology) 2. Salvation—Seventh-day Adventists.
3. Seventh-day Adventists—Doctrines. I. Title.

BX6154.D57 2003
234—dc21   2002193145

03 04 05 06 07 • 5 4 3 2 1

Dedication

For
Jan, Michael, Herb, Mavis, Reatha, Randy,
Vivienne Sue, Donna, Chip, and Judy
Fellow Travelers on the Road to Forever

*"I am writing this to you so that you may know
that you have eternal life—you that believe in the Son of God"
(1 John 5:13, TEV).*

Acknowledgments

I want to acknowledge, and with great gratitude, the many tributaries that have fed the river of thought now flowing through these pages. I wish I could remember all those who have fed my mind through the years—and they have been many, especially on the subject of this book. But I can remember with appreciation beyond words those who have read some or most of these chapters. Their own Christian insights have sharpened my mind with even clearer explanations of the joy of salvation—Jack Blanco, Russell Holt, Oliver Jacques, Bob Kyte, Jerry Moon, Ray Roth, Ted Wilson, and Kenneth Wood. Words cannot express my gratitude for my local church, Meadow Vista, California, for its warmth, dynamics, and personal suggestions after hearing these thoughts from the pulpit. And then, of course, Norma, my soulmate and amazing proofreader, who finds *non sequiturs* and misplaced commas after I think everything is "ready to go"!

Contents

CHAPTER ONE

Uncomfortable Questions

Has a friend ever asked you, "Are you saved?"

Did the question make you uncomfortable? How did you answer? Did you stumble and stammer—partly from modesty, partly from the knowledge that nothing is really settled until probation closes?

If you didn't say quickly, "Yes, I am saved!"—your friend would ask another question: "You mean you don't have any assurance that if Jesus came tonight, you would be saved?"

And if your friend is really sharp, he or she would continue, "You believe that you must do something to add to what Jesus has done for you—and you never know if you have done enough. Right?"

These are not mere academic questions.

I am a seasoned Adventist. I've been an Adventist since my early teens. I read my way into the joy of salvation. Through the writings of Ellen White I discovered a fresh understanding of the Bible and how Jesus was my Friend as well as my Savior and Lord. I am profoundly grateful for my college years at Atlantic Union College, for unforgettable years as a pastor, a college teacher and administrator, an editor, and an author of many articles and books.

But there have been times, in spite of my joy of salvation, when certain questions would haunt me: If probation closed today, would I be saved? Or, If I should die tonight, would I be in the first resurrection?

That sounds like a disconnect between my head and my heart, doesn't it? On the one hand, a joy of salvation; on the other, an unease regarding present salvation! Was something wrong with my theology? What did I not understand? What about the dark side of the investigative judgment when my name would "come up"? On top of all that, I knew that Ellen White had said that we should never say, "I am saved" (see *Selected Messages,* book 1, page 314; *Revival and Beyond,* page 41, etc.)! So what did I do for years? I put her statements and my fogginess regarding "being saved" way back on the top shelf—and turned to the business of the day!

As time went on, however, I looked at that top shelf again and again because I discovered that many others were having the same uncertainty. And worse—they were losing their sense of a saving relationship with Jesus. The thoughts in this book summarize my study and what I have been sharing with others on this topic through the years.

But I have another reason for writing this book. I recently received a letter from a long-time friend, a distinguished scholar, who, in his late seventies, feels he does not have the assurance of salvation! This man has an extensive Adventist heritage; both grandparents were church members before 1900. I will share only parts of his letter. He writes:

> We kids were brought up as pretty good SDAs, never using "gee" or "gosh" or "darn" or "heck" or such words, never eating meat, always being ready for the Sabbath at sundown Friday, reciting our memory verses for the quarter, attending camp meeting in the summers, reading the MV reading-course books, and doing the usual things SDAs did. Looking back, our parents were wise, kind, loving, and in most ways as good parents as anyone could ask for. As kids we used to end our prayers, "Help us to be good so we can be saved when Jesus comes."
>
> To skip a lot of ground . . . I think I became too religious. I used to wonder if I was good enough to be saved. . . . I saw the pictures of recording angels writing the record of the minutiae of our lives in ponderous books. I went through numerous weeks of prayer in academy and college and listened to testimonies such as, "I am determined to get the victory over my besetting sins." I gave such testimonies myself, and six months later at another week of prayer we would be making the same resolves and realizing we were just as far as before from living the "victorious life." One of the most awesome and scary things I heard over and over again was that the investigative judgment has been going

on since 1844, and by now they must be very close to deciding on my name for all eternity. "What more," I wondered, "could I do?" . . .

For years I would see a meeting on TV, maybe Billy Graham, and envy the people thronging there. They were happy, praising God for His salvation. They were thanking God for saving them! But then I would remember Ellen White. We were never to say "I am saved," and I would sink back in my misery. I finally admitted to myself that I devoutly wished I had been born a Baptist or something. Then I could come out into the sunlight and be a happy child of God. I used to fantasize that if I could just meet Jesus personally as He was on this earth, I would run and bow down before Him and tell Him I wanted to be a real Christian, but that I didn't know if I was one. I would tell Him that I wanted to serve Him and that I wanted the assurance that He loved me and would save me. Maybe He would even tell me, "Yes, I have saved you, and feel free to believe it!" . . .

I'm 79 now, and I hope for a few months or years of fellowship with Jesus my Savior, no longer separated by a gloomy cloud of salvation by works.

Don't you feel like weeping when you read this letter? What's going on, in this dear friend's life? Is it possible that you may feel that he is speaking for you? That, after years of faithful church attendance and reading many books, you still have no assurance of salvation? Or, as Paul expressed it, no "assurance of faith" (Hebrews 10:22)?

Somehow, in all his reading of the Bible and Ellen White (and he is a scholar), he did not get a clear picture of the plan of salvation. Nor, it seems, did he have a clear picture of the character of God. When he read Ellen White, he, apparently, saw only black clouds, not the noonday sun.

Where would you start in answering this letter? Your children, your parents, your friends—or you yourself—may be looking for the answers that my elderly friend is looking for.

Perhaps we all have looked with uncertainty at questions such as:

- How can I have assurance that I am saved today?
- If I should die tonight, do I know that I would be in the first resurrection?

Perhaps we also should ask:

- Would I rather die than sin?
- Can I be trusted with eternal life?
- Am I following known duty—the light I have?
- Do I have a saving relationship with Jesus?

Much of my friend's concerns (and perhaps yours as well) zero in on his reading of Ellen White (although the Bible, for him, also seemed to be clouded, obscuring a clear picture of the character of God). So to find some answers we should begin where Ellen White began—listening to the Bible.

CHAPTER TWO

Genuine Assurance Now

Jesus came to this world primarily to tell the truth about God (see John 14:9). He was not as Satan had made Him out to be.[1] God is not the cosmic cop in our rear-view mirror. He is not the "harsh, exacting" bookkeeper whose chief concern is keeping an accurate record of our sins. He is not the severe, revengeful judge that appears so often in Christian art and sermons. His chief goal and primary attitude toward us is not to condemn us, but to redeem us (see John 3:17-21).

How do I know all this? Because Jesus said so. Because when you see Jesus you are seeing God, our heavenly Father (see John 14:9). Jesus made it clear in many ways that the " 'Father Himself loves you' " (John 16:27). Further, Jesus calls us His friends, not His servants (see John 15:14, 15).

So what did Jesus say about our assurance of salvation? He tells us that we can know with certainty that we are in a saving relationship with Him *today!*

- " 'In very truth, anyone who gives heed to what I say and puts his trust in him who sent me has hold of eternal life, and does not come up for judgment, but has already passed from death to life' " (John 5:24, NEB).
- " 'The one who comes to Me, I will by no means cast out' " (John 6:37).
- " 'Most assuredly, I say to you, he who believes in [has faith in] Me has everlasting life' " (John 6:47).

- " 'I give them eternal life, and they shall never perish; neither shall anyone snatch them out of My hand. . . . No one is able to snatch them out of My Father's hand. I and My Father are one' " (John 10:28-30).
- " 'If anyone hears My words and does not believe [have faith], I do not judge him; for I did not come to judge the world but to save the world' " (John 12:47).

Unfortunately through the years, these words of Jesus have been strangely forgotten. I remember a Greek Orthodox church a few miles from Athens, not because of its ancient architecture, but because of its magnificent, domed ceiling high above the altar. The solid gold mosaic, providing a background for the face of Jesus, was dazzling. But I gasped in dismay when I looked into His face— a glowering frown was all that worshipers had seen of God for many centuries. For centuries, most of them could not read, and Bibles were scarce if they could. Therefore, the sculptures of biblical characters, the paintings, the exquisite mosaics—all these provided the basis for their "Bible" knowledge. No wonder, with a fearful God to worship—an arbitrary, exacting judge or scorekeeper— that worshipers fastened their eyes and hopes on Holy Mary, our Lord's mother or on His earthly father, Saint Joseph, when they prayed, knowing that even a frowning Jesus would listen kindly to His parents.

This is the kind of God that Satan has made Him out to be—frightening and harsh. Of course, in reaction, theologians have often portrayed God as a cosmic lover who, one way or another, no matter how long it takes, will ultimately save everyone. Of Him, they say, "love never fails."

Neither picture of God is correct, as Jesus made clear by word and example. Jesus described our heavenly Father, not as the arbitrary judge, not as the cosmic cop, not as the exacting bookkeeper, but as the waiting Father,[2] as the involved Parent.

In His unforgettable parable of the two sons and the patiently waiting Father, Jesus gave us not only blueprints of two kinds of men and women, but also a picture of God that incinerates all of Satan's lies about Him. Strange as it may seem, most of the sermons and books explaining this parable focus on the wasteful, irresponsible son, and sometimes on the other son who played it safe.

However, the primary point of the parable, it seems to me, is the same as that of the two preceding parables in which Jesus was giving a picture of God that the Pharisees never dreamed of. The devoted

Shepherd, the diligent Housewife, and the waiting Father belong to one giant mosaic depicting certain facets of a very wonderful heavenly Father.

Most people have heard these three stories told many times. But the grand theme of each story gets lost when we focus on the lost sheep, lost coin, and lost son. Granted, Jesus gives us all hope when we consider how we all have been, at times, the sheep, the coin, and the son. But when we read these parables, we should look at the main character and shout, "God is like that! Why should we ever doubt?"

Where do we find Jesus comparing our heavenly Father to the cosmic cop or the arrogant judge or the vengeful bookkeeper? Nowhere! So why should we?

Of course, we should take a long look at the wasteful son as if we were looking into a mirror. Or it may be the doing-everything-right son that we see in the mirror! But those thoughts belong to another book.

Our thoughts are brought back to the Father, the One around whom the story really turns. What brought the wasteful son to his senses?[3] Was it the stench of the pigpen? Was it the loathing of his "fair-weather" friends? Was it the filthy barn where he slept? Was it the gnawing hunger, day and night?

No, it was homesickness. "I remember Dad whistling into the sunrise," he said to himself, "singing as he milked the cows. I remember how he taught me to drive the oxen and to ride my own favorite horse. I remember those strong hands folded in prayer before each meal. I remember how patient Dad was when I broke the plow by trying to go too fast. I remember the sad shadow on Dad's face when he caught me lying. I remember the far-away look on his face when he gave me my so-called inheritance. And the arm around my shoulders when I left home. And his last wave before I turned the far corner."

No, it wasn't his empty pocketbook, his empty stomach, or his empty pride that brought the wasteful son to his senses—it was his memory of home and of his father that led him to repentance (see Romans 2:4). He had learned through bitter circumstances that he was the most free when he was with his father. He left his father only to find that he was soon chained by sensual gratifications, by the lies required to maintain his veneer, and by the addictions that dragged him to a pigpen.

When Jesus calls us to repentance, He doesn't try to make us even more disgusted with ourselves. He rings the bell of homesickness. He clears our vision so that we can see that our heavenly Father has never shut the front door and even now is standing at the gate waiting for us "to come to ourselves." Of course, a picture of our heavenly Father and home does make us more disgusted with ourselves, but it becomes a healthy disgust! We must get rid of it, and the sooner the better!

Furthermore, when Jesus talks about repentance, and especially in this parable, He does not couch His invitation with "Repent, dear ones, or you will burn in hellfire!" No, He says, "Repent, for yours is the kingdom of heaven!" Jesus always keeps our eyes on something better and the promise that He will help us get there!

I am emphasizing this parable because I think the story of the waiting father was given primarily for those who once knew the sweet taste of the Father's home. Prayer was a delight to them, and the Scriptures a daily pleasure. But somehow all that has faded under the stress of life—unconsciously perhaps, but still so far away.

Some readers may feel that Satan seems to be winning, throwing up one distraction after another until even the thought of being saved seems so uncertain. You may feel you are in your own "far country," far from your heavenly Father. In your quiet moments, you feel your misery, your despair.

Perhaps the only solid fact in your life is your memory, faded as it may be at the moment, that Jesus and the heavenly Father are there for you, ringing the bell of homesickness. Just as the waiting father embraced the wasteful son, so the heavenly Father already has His arms outstretched for you, waiting for you to "come to yourself."

Of course you feel guilt—as did the returning son. But you, too, can be smothered by the Father's embrace and His tears. Don't wait until you can pull yourself together before telling Him you are coming home—for that is impossible. He alone can turn your world right side up! He is the only One who can clear up the clouds in your life. Problems with relationships, with children, with your work, with your deep-grained addictions, with your anger (even though you may be right), with your self-satisfaction—all that is on your heavenly Father's agenda to work out. All you are to do is to fold yourselves in His everlasting arms and let Him work out the details. He is very good at what He does. And He can start even as you finish reading this chapter!

If Satan whispers—so logically—that you have gone too far this time or that you have wasted too many years, throw in his face our Lord's own words, " 'The one who comes to Me I will by no means cast out' " (John 6:37). In fact, the very thoughts you are now thinking have been aroused by the grace of the Holy Spirit, wanting you to consciously accept the wide open arms of your heavenly Father. He wants you to be saved *now!* Sense it! Believe it as much as you believe that Jesus died on the cross for you!

The waiting Father wants you to accept His greatest gift—the assurance that He has never shut the front door, the assurance that He never gives up on you, the assurance that appeals to your head and heart.

Everyone who joins the innumerable multitude around the throne of God will confess with eternal gratitude that God never gave up on them, that He rang the bell of homesickness until they "came to themselves." And they will never finish thanking Jesus for taking the risk in becoming a man so that this demented world could get a clear picture of God as the cosmic Lover, the waiting Father, the great Risk Taker.

No one outside the gates, will say that they never heard the bell of homesickness or never saw the light left on for them. Everyone has seen enough light to be saved (see John 1:9; Romans 2:14, 15).

In our next chapter we will briefly examine those hellish traps that "those outside the gates" fell into. They thought they had believed and done enough to be saved. What went wrong?

---

[1] "Satan led men to conceive of God as a being whose chief attribute is stern justice,—one who is a severe judge, a harsh, exacting creditor. He pictured the Creator as a being who is watching with jealous eye to discern the errors and mistakes of men, that He may visit judgments upon them. It was to remove this dark shadow, by revealing to the world the infinite love of God, that Jesus came to live among men" (Ellen G. White, *Steps to Christ*, p. 11).

[2] We are all indebted to Helmut Thielicke for this winsome phrase.

[3] " 'He came to himself' " (Luke 15:17).

CHAPTER THREE

False Assurance

With so much theological confusion in all denominations regarding *who* will be saved, it is always safe to listen to Jesus. Surely we shouldn't set Paul against Jesus—or John or Peter—and then say, "Take your pick! Who do you like best?" I have found it much safer when perplexity reigns, whatever the subject, to go back to my baseline and ask, "What did Jesus say?" I am a Christian today, not primarily because of what Ezekiel or Paul has written, but because of what I know about Jesus Christ and what *He* taught.

> "Not everyone who says to Me, 'Lord, Lord,' shall enter the kingdom of heaven, but he who does the will of My father in heaven. Many will say to Me in that day, 'Lord, Lord, have we not prophesied in Your name, cast out demons in Your name, and done many wonders in Your name?' And then I will declare to them, 'I never knew you; depart from Me, you who practice lawlessness' " (Matthew 7:21-23).

Jesus says that in the final judgment, many will be lost while believing that they are saved. How can that be? *They lived with a false assurance of salvation!*

Luke added further insights regarding Jesus' warning against false assurance:

> And He said to them, "Strive to enter through the narrow gate, for many, I say to you, will seek to enter and will not be

able. When once the Master of the house has risen up and shut the door, and you begin to stand outside and knock at the door, saying, 'Lord, Lord, open for us,' and He will answer and say to you, 'I do not know you, where you are from,' then you will begin to say, 'We ate and drank in Your presence, and You taught in our streets.' But He will say, 'I tell you I do not know you, where you are from. Depart from Me, all you workers of iniquity' " (Luke 13:23-27).

What is going on here? How can Jesus not "know" them? Of course, He knows them as He knows everyone who has ever lived. A better translation would be, "I never recognized you for what you said you were." And that word, *iniquity,* more accurately means "lawlessness," "lack of conformity with law." These individuals had the right words, but not the right life! They had the words, but not the music! They wanted salvation on their terms, not on their Master's terms. They wanted grace without responsibility. They wanted some kind of short-cut to salvation without going through the door of "the obedience of faith" (Romans 16:26). They diluted faith and substituted it for obedience.

In other words, here Jesus is giving us all a clear heads-up. Salvation is more than just saying the right words. Salvation is a matter of lining up our lives with the way God runs the universe. Our assurance of salvation rests on more than playing church or upon what others may say about our wonderful good deeds.

Paul understood the problem of false assurance when he wrote, "Examine yourselves as to whether you are in the faith. Prove your own selves" (2 Corinthians 13:5).

Ellen White echoed Paul:

> Deal truly with your own soul. Be as earnest, as persistent, as you would be if your mortal life were at stake. This is a matter to be settled between God and your own soul, settled for eternity. A supposed hope, and nothing more, will prove your ruin. . . . Desires for goodness and holiness are right as far as they go; but if you stop here, they will avail nothing. Many will be lost while hoping and desiring to be Christians. They do not come to the point of yielding the will to God.[1]

Peter, who went to the brink before he finally found himself, wrote: "Therefore, brethren, be even more diligent to make your call and election sure, for if you do these things you will never stumble"

(2 Peter 1:10). It seems that Ellen White's favorite scripture was Peter's first chapter in his second letter—she preached and wrote on it so much. She prized it as a clear picture of how to gain and maintain the assurance of salvation. After quoting verse 10 she wrote:

> We need not have a supposed hope, but an assurance. To make our calling and election sure is to follow the Bible plan to closely examine ourselves, to make strict inquiry whether we are indeed converted, whether our minds are drawn out after God and heavenly things, our wills renewed, our whole souls changed. To make our calling and election sure requires far greater diligence than many are giving to this important matter. "For if ye do these things"—live on the plan of addition, growing in grace and the knowledge of our Lord Jesus Christ—ye shall mount up, step by step, the ladder Jacob saw, and "ye shall never fall: for so an entrance shall be ministered unto you abundantly into the everlasting kingdom of our Lord and Savior Jesus Christ."[2]

What have we learned? That Jesus and the apostles knew the difference between true and false assurance. *False assurance means believing something that is not so!* It is the difference between the wise and the foolish bridesmaids. Both were "good and regular members" of the church. Both were "believers" who knew their Bibles. Both were eager for the Advent. Both were confident that they would be "saved." But for the wise, biblical principles had molded their lives; the Holy Spirit had transformed them into trusting, obedient, Christ-reflecting people. The foolish lulled their hearts into a false security. Their religion had become respectable, but they had only a "form of godliness . . . denying its power" (2 Timothy 3:5). For the foolish, daily fellowship with Jesus became an unknown experience. And they heard the saddest words that men and women will ever hear, "I do not know you—I do not know you for whom you say you are" (Matthew 7:23; see also Matthew 25:12).

Those tragic words remind us of our Lord's earlier and searing distinction between those who "say" they are saved and those who are living in a "saved relationship" with Him: " 'Not everyone who says to Me, "Lord, Lord," shall enter the kingdom of heaven, but he who does the will of My Father in heaven' " (Matthew 7:21). The test of genuine assurance, the acid test of sincerity, is not our words, but our actions, our willingness to let the Holy Spirit transform us into happy candidates for heaven.

It is hard to overlook Ezekiel's warning: " 'They come to you [Ezekiel] as people do, they sit before you as My people, and they hear your words, but they do not do them; for with their mouth they show much love, but their hearts pursue their own gain' " (Ezekiel 33:31). In other words, some people believe that they are right, when they are wrong. John echoed Ezekiel: "He who says, 'I know Him,' and does not keep His commandments, is a liar, and the truth is not in him" (1 John 2:4).

Those who say, "Only believe; only believe," have not heard the everlasting gospel. They are trapped in a limited gospel. They want Jesus as their Savior, but not as their Ruler. They have been told that grace accepts them as sinners; they have not been told that grace does not leave sinners where grace finds them. They have not understood the depth of sin and how God's love cannot overlook sin—it must be dealt with.[3]

They seem never to have heard that from "the throne of grace . . . we may obtain mercy and find grace to help in time of need" (Hebrews 4:16). The everlasting gospel promises both pardon and power,[4] both "mercy and . . . grace to help in time of need."

To plead for pardon only without asking for divine power to forsake the sins for which we ask forgiveness, is to walk down the slippery road to presumption.[5] And, it will result, ultimately, in finding ourselves among those to whom Jesus says, "I don't recognize you for whom you say you are."

Let's listen to the apostle John as he avoided the trap of presumptuous assurance on his journey into genuine assurance.

---

[1] *Steps to Christ*, pp. 35, 47, 48.

[2] *Manuscript Releases*, vol. 19, pp. 351, 352.

[3] "This goody-goody religion that makes light of sin and that is forever dwelling upon the love of God to the sinner encourages the sinner to believe that God will save him while he continues in sin and he knows it to be sin. This is the way that many are doing who profess to believe present truth. The truth is kept apart from their life, and that is the reason it has no more power to convict and convert the soul" (Ellen G. White, *Selected Messages*, bk. 3, p. 155).

[4] See Ellen G. White, *Education*, p. 36.

[5] When John wrote 1 John 1:9, he quoted Proverbs 28:13, but not completely— "He who covers his sins will not prosper. But whoever confesses and forsakes them will have mercy." Many have read only "confession" when they seek God's plan, God's pardon, which obscures the reality of how God intends to deal with our sins. Forsaking the sins one is confessing is implicit in John's thoughts when he adds that God is "faithful and just to forgive us our sins and to *cleanse us from all unrighteousness.*"

CHAPTER FOUR

How John Found Genuine Assurance

In his first letter, John explains why and how all Christians should be as sure of their salvation as he was of his own. In fact, that was the purpose of his first letter: "This letter is to assure you that you have eternal life. It is addressed to those who give their allegiance to the Son of God" (1 John 5:13, NEB).

Here John reviews his Christian experience and is most forthright as to how all Christians may have assurance:

> Here is the test by which we can make sure that we know him: do we keep [literally, make a habit of keeping] his commands? The man who says, "I know him," while he disobeys his commands, is a liar and a stranger to the truth (1 John 2:3, NEB).

> Here is the test by which we can make sure that we are in him: whoever claims to be dwelling in him, binds himself to live as Christ himself lived (1 John 2:6, NEB).

> And yet again it is a new command that I am giving you— new in the sense that the darkness is passing and the real light already shines. Christ has made this true, and it is true in your own experience (1 John 2:8, NEB).

> We for our part have crossed over from death to life; this we know, because we love our brothers (1 John 3:14, NEB).

This is how we may know that we belong to the realm of truth, and convince ourselves in his sight that even if our conscience condemns us, God is greater than our conscience and knows all (1 John 3:20, NEB).

Here is the proof that we dwell in him and he dwells in us: he has imparted his Spirit to us (1 John 4:13, NEB).

He who believes in the Son of God has this testimony in his own heart, but he who disbelieves God, makes him out to be a liar, by refusing to accept God's own witness to his Son. The witness is this: that God has given us eternal life, and that this life is found in his Son. He who possesses the Son has life indeed; he who does not possess the Son of God has not that life (1 John 5:10-12, NEB).

What shall we make of all this? John is emphatically clear; there are no "perhap's" and "maybe's"! Christians may have the assurance of salvation *now* because of certain undeniable truths that they have learned in *their own experience.*

- When they choose to obey whatever light that comes their way, continuing to walk into the light as it ever unfolds the future (see Proverbs 4:18).
- When they "live as Christ himself lived" (1 John 2:6).
- When their assurance is based, not on some theological or philosophical argument, but on their own experience as they reflect on the historical facts.
- When they experience the validating, guiding voice of the Holy Spirit.
- When their heart experience is validated and manifested in a new kind of love for others.

But John does more. He clearly explains the basis of his own assurance. In other words, he tells us why he is so sure that he has salvation here and now: In fact, the first four verses of John's first letter are, to me, some of the most amazing thoughts in the entire Bible! I have thrown myself upon them at some very important moments in my life. I think I read them more often than any other part of the Bible during my doctoral program in theology. Let's listen to John:

It was there from the beginning; we have heard it; we have seen it with our own eyes; we looked upon it, and felt it with our own hands; and it is of this we tell. Our theme is the word of life. This life was made visible; we have seen it and bear our testimony; we here declare to you the eternal life which dwelt with the Father and was made visible to us. What we have seen and heard we declare to you, so that you and we together may share in a common life, that life which we share [present tense] with the Father and his Son Jesus Christ. And we write this in order that the joy of us all may be complete (1 John 1:1-4, NEB).

John's assurance of salvation rested on his own experience as he responded to His Lord's words and life. What makes John's experience even more relevant for me today are Ellen White's comments regarding how we can duplicate John's experience.

After emphasizing how the youth may "make the word of God the food of mind and soul" and how this habit may mold "the daily experience in practical life," making "the Savior . . . a daily companion and friend," she wrote:

> Thus through faith they come to know God by an experimental [experiential] knowledge. They have proved for themselves the reality of His word, the truth of His promises. They have tasted, and they know that the Lord is good. The beloved John had a knowledge gained through his own experience. He could testify: [Quoted 1 John 1:1-3.]
>
> So everyone may be able, through his own experience, to "set his seal to this, that God is true." John 3:33, A.R.V. He can bear witness to that which he himself has seen and heard and felt of the power of Christ. He can testify: "I needed help, and I found it in Jesus. Every want was supplied, the hunger of my soul was satisfied; the Bible is to me the revelation of Christ. I believe in Jesus because He is to me a divine Savior. I believe the Bible because I have found it to be the voice of God to my soul."[1]

These lines must be read slowly, again and again. They form the anatomy of what Paul called, "the assurance of faith" (Hebrews 10:22). Here John explains how the assurance of faith is built up through the years.

It is more than interesting, however, that John has said all this without once using the word, "faith." The only time John used the Greek word *pistis* ("faith") is in 1 John 5:4—and never in the Gospel of John! "Faith" (*pistis*) is Paul's favorite word; "abide," (*meno*) is John's.[2]

John uses *meno,* "to abide," eleven times in his Gospel and twenty-six times in his letters. "Abide in Christ" is John's equivalent to Paul's "to be in Christ."

For John, "abiding in Christ," emphasizes the experiential fellowship that he enjoyed with Jesus for more than three years and the intense experience he had shared with Jesus since His ascension. In a later chapter we will discuss John's and Paul's use of the verb, *pisteuo* which in the Greek always means, "to have faith." The tragedy of the centuries is that this Greek word for "faith in action" is almost always translated "to believe," an altogether different direction than what the New Testament writers intended. More about this later.

What have we learned thus far? John's profound, unshakable certainty that Jesus was His Lord and that he had the assurance of salvation may be ours in the same way that John built his faith. Remember, it was only after Calvary that John and the other disciples truly had faith in Jesus as their Savior and Ruler.

This assurance is built on more than historical information. John bowed to the Jesus of history and made Him the Christ of experience. And he bore witness, validated by the Holy Spirit, that everything Jesus said and did was light in the darkness of his own life. He recalled the words of Jesus, listened to the prompting of the Holy Spirit, and wrote all this out in his Gospel. The written word and the inner word became the voice of God to his soul. And so it may be with us.

Day and night, our hearts and heads will find the certitude we long for! We find it exactly the way John found it. By joining the written word with the inner word of the Spirit and saying "Yes" to all that He is opening up to us. The assurance of faith gets deeper as the years go by. Just ask John!

---

[1] *The Ministry of Healing,* p. 461.

[2] This fact alone should caution against building a theological doctrine on one word. Perhaps John would have looked at what Paul refers to as "righteousness by faith" and called the same event/experience, "righteousness by abiding."

CHAPTER FIVE

Ellen White on Genuine Assurance

In so many ways, over so many years, Ellen White breathed out her own assurance that Jesus was her Savior and Friend. In fact, hundreds of thousands of her readers have affirmed that they found Jesus to be their Savior and Friend because of her lucid, insightful sermons and written messages.

In *Steps to Christ*, now published in about 150 languages and dialects, she speaks directly to our main question of whether we have the right to expect present salvation:

> Satan is ready to steal away the blessed assurances of God. He desires to take every glimmer of hope and every ray of light from the soul; but you must not permit him to do this. Do not give ear to the tempter, but say, "Jesus has died that I might live. He loves me, and wills not that I should perish. I have a compassionate heavenly Father; and although I have abused His love, though the blessings He has given me have been squandered, I will arise, and go to my Father, and say, 'I have sinned against heaven, and before Thee, and am no more worthy to be called Thy son: make me as one of Thy hired servants.'" The parable tells you how the wanderer will be received: "*When he was yet a great way off*, his father saw him, and had compassion, and ran, and fell on his neck, and kissed him." Luke 15:18-20.
>
> But even this parable, tender and touching as it is, comes short of expressing the infinite compassion of the heavenly Father. The Lord declares by His prophet, "I have loved thee

with an everlasting love: *therefore with loving-kindness have I drawn thee*" (Jeremiah 31:3). While the sinner is yet far from the Father's house, wasting his substance in a strange country, the Father's heart is yearning over him; and every longing awakened in the soul to return to God is but the tender pleading of His Spirit, wooing, entreating, drawing the wanderer to his Father's heart of love.[1]

Typical of many articles she wrote for the church paper, *Review and Herald,* is the following excerpt. It is part of a camp meeting report in which she is urging the ministers to come close to the people, helping them to unite an experiential relationship with Jesus with the special truths of the Advent message. She appeals to the ministers to avoid "oratorical sermons." She wanted people to hear clear messages about Jesus as their living Savior who not only pardons but empowers His believers to become living witnesses to the power of the gospel:

Simple faith in the atoning blood can save my soul; and with John, I must call the attention of all to the Lamb of God, which taketh away the sin of the world. Jesus has saved me, though I had nothing to present to him, and could only say,

"In my hand no price I bring,
Simply to thy cross I cling."

Never did a sinner seek the Savior with the whole heart, but that the Savior was found of him. Every soul who trusts in Jesus can say,

"Jesus as I am, Thou wilt receive,
Wilt welcome, pardon, cleanse, relieve;
Because thy promise I believe,
O Lamb of God, I come, I come."

We may claim the blessed assurance, "I have blotted out, as a thick cloud, thy transgressions." Thy "sins, which are many, are forgiven." O, how precious, how refreshing, is the sunlight of God's love! The sinner may look upon his sin-stained life, and say, "Who is he that condemneth? It is Christ that died." "When sin abounded, grace did much more abound." Christ, the Restorer, plants a new principle of life in the soul, and that plant grows and produces fruit. The grace of Christ purifies while it pardons, and fits men for a holy heaven. We are to grow in grace and in the knowledge of our Lord Jesus Christ, until we reach the full stature of men and women in Christ.[2]

In her world-acclaimed life of Christ, Ellen White recognized that to tell a person to have more faith is often just one more burden to lay on a struggling man or woman. That is exactly the problem—they don't feel they have any faith to give! What then? Listen:

> It is faith that connects us with heaven, and brings us strength for coping with the powers of darkness. In Christ, God has provided means for subduing every sinful trait, and resisting every temptation, however strong. But many feel that they lack faith, and therefore they remain away from Christ. Let these souls, in their helpless unworthiness, cast themselves upon the mercy of their compassionate Savior. Look not to self, but to Christ. He who healed the sick and cast out demons when He walked among men is the same mighty Redeemer today. Faith comes by the word of God. Then grasp His promise, "Him that cometh to Me I will in no wise cast out." John 6:37. Cast yourself at His feet with the cry, "Lord, I believe; help *Thou* mine unbelief." You can never perish while you do this—never.[3]

The open secret is that we are not to trust in our faith, but in God's faithfulness. Our feelings are too often misinterpreted as our "faith." Too often we misquote Mark 11:22 and fall apart because Jesus seems to be asking us to do the seemingly impossible: "Have faith in God." That's the problem! If we don't sense we have faith, how can we "have faith"?

But the literal translation of Mark 11:22 reads: "Keep holding on to God's faithfulness." That is the only way that I have found to survive when I meet with situations that are beyond me, especially when I am tired and stressed with multiple tasks, all demanding immediate attention. I think also of Hebrews 10:23—"Let us hold fast the confession of our hope without wavering, for *He who promised is faithful*" (emphasis supplied).

In 1894, Ellen White wrote to a dear friend who was in great physical suffering, a mature Christian who felt smothered by those satanic shadows that seem to have eclipsed the sun:

> Satan will try to cloud your mind with the thought that Jesus does not love you. He will try to make you believe that

you are unworthy of being acknowledged before the Father as His child, but do not believe his suggestions for a single moment. I know that the Lord loves you and that there will be souls in the kingdom of God that will be saved as the result of your unselfish labor, your steadfast adherence to the faith.

When Satan comes in with his suggestions, look unto Jesus and say, "Who is he that condemneth? It is Christ who died, yea rather, that is risen again, who is even at the right hand of God, who also maketh intercession for us" (Romans 8:34). Only think of this, my sister. Christ is the one who has died for you, who has purchased you with His own precious blood. Will He permit those whom He values so highly to walk alone? Nay, He will not. The apostle continues, "Who shall separate us from the love of Christ? Shall tribulation?" (Romans 8:35). Nay. Jesus bore all this in my behalf when He accepted humanity, and He bore it in order that I might not perish, but have everlasting life. Will He who has done all this for you be indifferent to you when it is difficult for you to engage in the warfare and to fight the good fight of faith? You are weak, and the trembling hand of faith can scarcely grasp the promises, but cannot you now say, "Lord, I am now too weak to use the weapons of warfare, but I can repose in Thee as my only hope. In Thee, and in Thee alone, my Redeemer, is my only hope of eternal life. Thou art my refuge"?

The message from God to me for you is "He that cometh unto me, I will in no wise cast out" (John 6:37). If you have nothing else to plead before God but this one promise from your Lord and Savior, you have the assurance that you will never, never be turned away. It may seem to you that you are hanging upon a single promise, but appropriate that one promise, and it will open to you the whole treasure house of the riches of the grace of Christ. Cling to that promise and you are safe. "He that cometh unto me I will in no wise cast out." Present this assurance to Jesus, and you are as safe as though inside the city of God.

You are not to examine your feelings and put any dependence upon your emotions, for they may be as varied as the wind, but take to your heart this one promise and you will find it a passport to all the rich treasures of heaven. You are precious to the heart of Christ and He speaks, saying unto you, "Come unto Me, all ye that labor and are heavy laden, and I will give you rest" (Matthew 11:28). There is no perhaps or maybe about this promise. The "I will" of Christ is an assurance that cannot be made any stronger. He speaks further, saying, "Take My yoke upon you, and learn of Me; for I am meek and lowly of heart: and ye shall find rest unto your souls. For My yoke is easy, and My burden is light" (Matthew 11:29, 30).

Now, my sister, Jesus wants you to believe in Him as your personal Savior, as One who can save unto the uttermost all who come unto God by Him. Your request made known unto God in the name of Jesus is ever acceptable to your heavenly Father. You have a right to appropriate the promises which you present to God in the name of Jesus, for the Father has committed to His Son the bounties of His grace to be dispensed to those who come unto Him asking in faith. . . .

My dear sister, Jesus will not leave you. He loves you with an everlasting love, and as you trust in Him your faith will grow and increase. The more you trust your Redeemer the more you will love Him. He is your friend in life or in death. He is the crown of your rejoicing. He is worthy of your fullest faith. All the sorrows and afflictions we suffer here only constitutes our discipline for a higher life, for through the appropriated grace of Christ trials will be the means whereby we shall be purified and fitted for heaven. Wait only upon God. Lean upon Him in entire dependence, for His everlasting arms hold you up and sustain you. Will not He who says that not a sparrow falls to the ground without the notice of your heavenly Father care for you who trust and love Him? Jesus knows every throb of pain, every throe of anguish and distress, and He will give you grace to endure your affliction in order that your faith fail not, whatever may be your suffering.

Dear Sister____, keep up good courage. Let not your heart be oppressed. You have been called upon to travel a thorny path, but Jesus is at your side to journey the rough road with you. He knows, He understands every woe, every sorrow of those who suffer. His heart beats in sympathy with the hearts of suffering humanity, and those who suffer most have most of His pity and sympathy. He is your best Friend. . . .

I would urge upon you, as a family, during the time when affliction is upon this beloved sister, that you all draw closer and closer in faith and confidence to Jesus. Talk cheerfully. Let not one jarring note be heard. Let no touch of sadness or gloom reveal itself on your countenances. Keep Jesus uplifted. Talk faith in Jesus and sing songs of faith.[4]

I have quoted her counsel at length because I know that many people, even those who have read Ellen White's theological books, such as the five volumes in the *Conflict* set, have never read any of her hundreds of letters such as this one sent to Lizzie Innes in 1894. Hundreds of people received this kind of spiritual nourishment throughout Ellen White's seventy-year ministry.

The reader can easily see how clear Ellen White was in urging the ministers assembled at the General Conference of 1883 in Battle Creek, Michigan, to experience assurance *now!* While counseling them to pray shorter prayers but with more earnestness, she said:

> I have listened to testimonies like this: "I have not the light that I desire; I have not the assurance of the favor of God." Such testimonies express only unbelief and darkness. Are you expecting that your merit will recommend you to the favor of God, and that you must be free from sin before you trust his power to save? If this is the struggle going on in your mind, I fear you will gain no strength, and will finally become discouraged. . . . Poor sinsick, discouraged soul, look and live. Jesus has pledged his word; He will save all who come unto him. Then let us come confessing our sins, bringing forth fruits meet for repentance.
>
> Jesus is our Savior today. He is pleading for us in the most holy place of the heavenly sanctuary, and He will forgive our sins. It makes all the difference in the world with us spiritually whether we rely upon God without doubt, as upon a sure foundation, or whether we are seeking to find some righteousness in ourselves before we come to Him. Look away from self to the Lamb of God, that taketh away the sin of the world. It is a sin to doubt. The least unbelief, if cherished in the heart, involves the soul in guilt, and brings great darkness and discouragement. It is saying that the Lord is false; that He will not do as He has promised; and He is greatly dishonored. Some have cherished doubts, discontent, and a disposition to be on the wrong side, until they love doubts, and seem to think it is praiseworthy to be on the side of the doubting. But when the believing ones shall receive the end of their faith, even the salvation of their souls, the doubting ones, who have sowed unbelief, will reap that which they have sown, and a pitiful, undesirable harvest it will be.
>
> Some seem to feel that they must be on probation, and must prove to the Lord that they are reformed before they can claim his blessing. But these dear souls may claim the blessing of God even now. They must have His grace, the spirit of Christ

to help their infirmities, or they cannot form Christian characters. Jesus loves to have us come to Him just as we are—sinful, helpless, dependent.[5]

In a sermon preached in Oakland, California, on November 7, 1891, Ellen White encouraged her listeners regarding present assurance:

> You are not to look to the future, thinking that at some distant day you are to be made holy; it is now that you are to be sanctified through the truth. . . . We are to receive the Holy Ghost. We have had an idea that this gift of God was not for such as we are, that the gift of the Holy Spirit was too sacred, too holy for us; but the Holy Spirit is the Comforter that Christ promised to His disciples. . . . Then let us cease to look to ourselves, but look to Him from whom all virtue comes. No one can make himself better, but we are to come to Jesus as we are, earnestly desiring to be cleansed from every spot and stain of sin, and receive the gift of the Holy Spirit. We are not to doubt His mercy, and say, "I do not know whether I shall be saved or not." By living faith we must lay hold of His promise, for He has said, "Though your sins be as scarlet, they shall be as white as snow, though they be red like crimson, they shall be as wool."
>
> How strange it seems that with all the assurances of God's love, with all the manifestation of His power in our behalf, many are cold and indifferent, even among those who profess to believe the truth for this time. They do not bear a ringing, living testimony to the praise of God, for their faith and love have diminished to a feeble flame. Oh, that we all might be baptized with the Holy Spirit. Oh, that we might be as vessels unto the Lord. We want to see all the folly weeded out of the hearts of those who profess to be followers of the Lord, that the joy of the Lord may come in.[6]

In an early morning talk to the General Conference delegates in 1901, Ellen White encouraged her hearers to reach out more diligently to Scandinavia, to the southern states, to New York City, and to raise the wages for our sanitarium workers. In the midst of her global review, she zoomed in on perhaps their greatest need—she did not want them to be in any doubt regarding their assurance of salvation. (Uppermost in everyone's mind was the "Holy Flesh" problem in Indiana where many believed that complete sanctification, that is, complete eradication of sin, was the condition for present assurance.):

Each one of you may know for yourself that you have a living Savior, that He is your helper and your God. You need not stand where you say, "I do not know whether I am saved." Do you believe in Christ as your personal Savior? If you do, then rejoice. We do not rejoice half as much as we should. This entire congregation should be filled with rejoicing because of the way in which God has been revealing himself in this meeting. God's power has been seen, and His salvation is still to be revealed to His people. I see in Jesus a wonderful power and strength, and I want you to see this. Then your hearts will be as humble as the heart of a little child. Then you will not quarrel over who shall have the highest place or the highest wages. Your question will be, "How can I best serve my Lord?"[7]

These assurances of present salvation in the writings of Ellen White can be multiplied hundreds of times. Just in case I have not made her consistent message clear enough, note the following from an 1884 article:

Some seem to feel that they must be on probation and must prove to the Lord that they are reformed before they can claim His blessing. But these dear souls may claim the blessing of God even now. They must have His grace, the spirit of Christ to help their infirmities, or they cannot form Christian characters. Jesus loves to have us come to Him just as we are—sinful, helpless, dependent. We claim to be children of the light, not of the night nor of darkness; what right have we to be unbelieving?[8]

But, what about those Ellen White statements that have caused perplexity for some, especially to my dear friend who wrote that letter I cited in the first chapter of this book? Let's look next at every possible "problem" statement in the writings of Ellen White that have been perplexing to some—statements that, unfortunately, have been sadly misused and misunderstood.

---

[1] Page 53, emphasis in original.
[2] *Review and Herald,* July 14, 1891.
[3] *The Desire of Ages,* p. 429, emphasis in original.
[4] *Manuscript Releases,* vol. 10, pp. 174–178.
[5] *Review and Herald,* April 22, 1884.
[6] *Signs of the Times,* April 4, 1892.
[7] *General Conference Bulletin,* April 10, 1901.
[8] *Review and Herald,* April 22, 1884.

Ellen White's Misused Statements

True, Ellen White wrote at least four statements that have caused much perplexity for those who wish for the assurance of salvation *now, today.* As we will soon see, each of these statements are misused when (1) taken out of their immediate context (that is, lifted out of the meaning of that particular document, whether a letter, book, or sermon) (2) lifted out of the historical context within which she wrote her warning.

First misused statement

After reviewing Peter's heady self-confidence a few hours before Calvary, Ellen White in that astonishingly profound book, *Christ's Object Lessons,* wrote:

> Peter's fall was not instantaneous, but gradual. Self-confidence led him to the belief that he was saved, and step after step was taken in the downward path, until he could deny his Master. Never can we safely put confidence in self or feel, this side of heaven, that we are secure against temptation. Those who accept the Savior, however sincere their conversion, should never be taught to say or to feel that they are saved. This is misleading. Every one should be taught to cherish hope and faith; but even when we give ourselves to Christ and know that He accepts us, we are not beyond the reach of temptation. . . .
>
> Those who accept Christ, and in their first confidence say, I am saved, are in danger of trusting to themselves. They lose

sight of their own weakness and their constant need of divine strength. They are unprepared for Satan's devices, and under temptation many, like Peter, fall into the very depths of sin. We are admonished, "Let him that thinketh he standeth, take heed lest he fall" (1 Cor. 10:12). Our only safety is in constant distrust of self, and dependence on Christ.[1]

What is going on here? It seems that Ellen White is very emphatic—don't say, "I am saved!" After reading her statements in the last chapter, are we now faced with contradictions? No, hardly! This is another example of why we must be careful with the rules of interpretation when we want to understand what others have written. Let's look closely at this passage:

- Everyone should cherish hope and faith and know that Christ accepts us [present tense].
- Everyone should resist self-confidence, thinking that we are secure against temptation.
- The phrase, "I am saved," is used in the context of thinking one is *eternally secure now.* No one is eternally secure (saved ultimately) until one's death or the Second Advent. As Jesus Himself said, " 'He who endures to the end shall be saved [ultimately]' " (Matthew 24:13).
- On this particular page in *Christ's Object Lessons* we have an excellent example of Ellen White's usual balance in stating gospel truths. On the one hand, Ellen White warns against self-confidence which leads to presumptuous assurance. (A false assurance confuses a person's daily sense of a saving relationship with Jesus and that person's ultimate salvation.) On the other hand, she is explicit with her encouragement—that in cherishing hope and faith, we should know that He accepts us now (present tense).

This remarkable skill in balancing warning with encouragement characterizes the writings of Ellen White.[2] If at any time we sense only warning, we can be sure that if we read on we will hear the encouragement. It is the principle of the ellipse that permeates her writings. Both foci are needed to understand the whole truth. Focusing on one foci alone breeds dismay, on one hand, or, presumptuous self-satisfaction, on the other.

Unfortunately, when one reads only portions of some of her letters in her nine-volume *Testimonies for the Church,* one may get the impression that she is mostly rebuke and condemnation. Rarely is that the conclusion when one reads the entire letter. Her contemporaries knew her as a faithful messenger of the Lord, who spoke as plainly as any biblical prophet but always within the larger context of encouragement.

Second misused statement

Our second illustration of a misused statement is found in a *Review and Herald* article for June 17, 1890 (reprinted in *Selected Messages,* book 1, pp. 314, 315):

> We are never to rest in a satisfied condition, and cease to make advancement, saying, "I am saved." When this idea is entertained, the motives for watchfulness, for prayers, for earnest endeavor to press onward to higher attainments, cease to exist. No sanctified tongue will be found uttering these words till Christ shall come, and we enter in through the gates into the city of God. Then, with the utmost propriety, we may give glory to God and to the Lamb for eternal deliverance. As long as man is full of weakness—for of himself he cannot save his soul—he should never dare to say, "I am saved.". . . .
>
> We should raise no human standard whereby to measure character. We have seen enough of what men call perfection here below. God's holy law is the only thing by which we can determine whether we are keeping His way or not. If we are disobedient, our characters are out of harmony with God's moral rule of government, and it is stating a falsehood to say, "I am saved." No one is saved who is a transgressor of the law of God, which is the foundation of His government in heaven and in earth.[3]

Again, what is Ellen White talking about in this article? She is looking at the problem of presumptuous assurance from a slightly different angle than our previous misused statement. For example:

- Presumptuous assurance wants to "rest in a satisfied condition and cease to make advancement."
- Presumptuous assurance is based on the popular assumption of "once saved, always saved," disregarding the many biblical warnings such as Hebrews 10:38 and Matthew 24:13.
- Presumptuous assurance, in terms of this article, is associated with those who teach that "the law of God is no longer binding upon the human family."

- Thus, saying, "I am saved," within the context of these pages is presumptuous assurance.

Third misused statement

Our third misused statement is clearly set within the historical context of an evangelical distortion of the gospel.[4] Ellen White wrote often and spoke frequently against the easy gospel wherein (1) character transformation was muted, and (2) a declaration of "only believe" contained the essential fact in one's salvation. This misunderstanding of the gospel declared that Jesus on the cross satisfied everything that has to do with our salvation; no interest is expressed in His work as our High Priest or in what is involved in the human response to His gift of salvation.

In her articles for the *Signs of the Times,* Ellen White wrote specifically with the general public in mind, knowing that her readers would recognize immediately the errors she was pointing out:

> The doctrine is now largely taught that the gospel of Christ has made the law of God of no effect; that by "believing" we are released from the necessity of being doers of the word. But this is the doctrine of the Nicolaitans, which Christ so unsparingly condemned. [Revelation 2:2-6, quoted]. . . .
>
> Those who are teaching this doctrine today have much to say in regard to faith and the righteousness of Christ; but they pervert the truth, and make it serve the cause of error. They declare that we have only to believe on Jesus Christ, and that faith is all-sufficient; that the righteousness of Christ is to be the sinner's credentials; that this imputed righteousness fulfils the law for us, and that we are under no obligation to obey the law of God. This class claim that Christ came to save sinners, and that He has saved them. "I am saved," they will repeat over and over again. But are they saved while transgressing the law of Jehovah?—No; for the garments of Christ's righteousness are not a cloak for iniquity. Such teaching is a gross deception, and Christ becomes to these persons a stumbling-block as He did to the Jews—to the Jews because they would not receive Him as their personal Savior; to these professed believers in Christ, because they separate Christ and the law, and regard faith as a substitute for obedience. They separate the Father and the Son, the Savior of the world. Virtually they teach, both by precept and example, that Christ, by His death, saves men in their transgressions.[5]

This reference looks at the "I am saved" problem from an obviously different angle than the two previous examples. Bad theology produces bad results. Satan is interested in any approach that will deflect the Christian's gaze and provide an instant assurance that all is well, when all is not well![6]

This passage teaches us that:

- Christians should not substitute faith for obedience; this is clear evidence that faith is misunderstood.
- Imputed righteousness is heaven-sent but cannot, of itself, fulfill the law for us.
- The garments of Christ's righteousness cover only confessed sins that sinners want cleansed from their lives—not unconfessed sins (iniquity).
- Presumptuous assurance expects salvation while knowingly transgressing God's law.

Fourth misused statement

Our fourth misused statement is understood clearly within the historical context of 1892 as well as the purpose of Ellen White's article in the *Review and Herald*. Here we also have the pleasure of seeing in close connection the balance, the ellipse of truth,[7] in how Ellen White sees opposite dangers in understanding truth:

> It is essential to have faith in Jesus, and to believe you are saved through him; but there is danger in taking the position that many do take in saying, "I am saved." Many have said: "You must do good works, and you will live;" but apart from Christ no one can do good works. Many at the present day say, "Believe, only believe, and live." Faith and works go together, believing and doing are blended. . . . Let no one take up with the delusion so pleasant to the natural heart, that God will accept of sincerity, no matter what may be the faith, no matter how imperfect may be the life. God requires of his child perfect obedience. . . .
>
> Through union with Christ, through acceptance of his righteousness by faith, we may be qualified to work the works of God, to be co-laborers with Christ. If you are willing to drift along with the current of evil, and do not cooperate with the heavenly agencies in restraining transgression in your family, and in the church, in order that everlasting righteousness may be brought in, you do not have faith. Faith works by love and

purifies the soul. Through faith the Holy Spirit works in the heart to create holiness therein; but this cannot be done unless the human agent will work with Christ. We can be fitted for heaven only through the work of the Holy Spirit upon the heart; for we must have Christ's righteousness as our credentials if we would find access to the Father. In order that we may have the righteousness of Christ, we need daily to be transformed by the influence of the Spirit, to be a partaker of the divine nature. It is the work of the Holy Spirit to elevate the taste, to sanctify the heart, to ennoble the whole man.[8]

- Could Ellen White be any clearer? "It is essential," she said, that we have a present sense of being saved.
- Presumptuous assurance seeks salvation in either of two ways: By trusting (1) that external obedience to God's law will assure salvation, or (2) that sincerity is equated with faith and thus, salvation is assured apart from obedience to God's law.[9]
- Genuine assurance rests, not on external obedience (because without the empowerment of grace, obedience may be mere legalism without character transformation).
- Genuine assurance (which is "essential") rests on genuine faith— that awesome blend of trust and obedience (believing and doing).[10]

What have we learned in this chapter? When one senses a problem or an apparent discrepancy in Ellen White's writings, it is a call to read further.

I have found every allegation charging Ellen White with contradictions to be unfounded when I have read her in context. In *Messenger of the Lord*, seven chapters are devoted to the rules of interpretation (hermeneutics). One of the basic principles listed there is that we must "include all that the prophet has said on the subject under discussion before coming to a conclusion." Another principle is that "every statement must be understood within its historical context. Time, place, and circumstances under which that statement was made must be studied in order to understand its meaning."[11]

The Bible and Ellen White are equally clear regarding how Christians are to maintain their saving relationship with Jesus. To this cheerful topic we turn next.

---

[1] Page 155.

[2] I am indebted to Dr. Jerry Moon, professor of church history, at the Seventh-day Adventist Theological Seminary for this insight and others in this book.

[3] Pages 314, 315.

[4] Most probably, in Ellen White's era, the primary message of the Plymouth Brethren, Southern Baptists, and emerging "Holiness" and/or charismatic denominations.

[5] *Signs of the Times*, February 25, 1897.

[6] "There are many who profess Christ, but who never become mature Christians. They admit that man is fallen, that his faculties are weakened, that he is unfitted for moral achievement, but they say that Christ has borne all the burden, all the suffering, all the self-denial, and they are willing to let him bear it. They say that there is nothing for them to do but to believe; but Christ said, 'If any man will come after me, let him deny himself, and take up his cross, and follow me' " *(Review and Herald*, June 17, 1890).

[7] The phrase, "the ellipse of truth," is a friendly way of describing the biblical truths. An ellipse has two foci, a circle has one. But the ellipse can be destroyed when one foci is muted or overemphasized at the expense of the other foci. For instance, which is more important, hydrogen or oxygen, when one wants a drink of water? When one listens to the everlasting gospel, pardon and power are the basic elements—or, as some say, justification and sanctification. Neither is more important than the other in the purpose of the gospel. Another way of stating the ellipse is to note the vital connection between mental belief and heart commitment in the Christian walk. The error of "only believe" is obvious when the limited gospel does not also place equal emphasis on the Holy Spirit's work in transforming the "believer."

[8] *Review and Herald*, November 1, 1892.

[9] Ellen White's letter to her husband from Salem, Oregon, in 1878, refers to a minister who "seeks to please his congregation, and tells them [that] young people must have pleasure; it is no harm to go to the theater and attend parties of pleasure and to dance. . . . The ministers tell the congregations they cannot keep the law; no man ever kept it or ever will keep it. What a theory! The wise and good God presents to His people a law that is to govern their actions which it is impossible for them to observe!" *(Manuscript Releases,* vol. 21, p. 243).

[10] See pp. 52–62.

[11] Herbert E. Douglass, *Messenger of the Lord* (Nampa, Idaho: Pacific Press Publishing Association, 1998), pp. 394, 395.

CHAPTER SEVEN

How to Maintain Genuine Assurance

Her sermon on September 19, 1891, was typical of Ellen White's many camp meeting sermons she preached from coast to coast, in a schedule that hardly a man today could match. Constantly she holds up the Christian's assurance within the goal of the gospel—preparing believers to live forever:

Now, some will tell you, and they will begin to reckon, and reckon, and reckon when the latter rain is coming. I would rather that you would reckon right now whether you have brought eternity into your reckoning concerning your individual self. Consider whether you have brought eternity daily to view. *If you are right with God today, you are ready if Christ should come today.* What we need is Christ formed within, the hope of glory. . . .

What we want to know is, Are you individually, daily preparing that you can unite with the family of heaven? Are you quarrelsome here? Are you finding fault with your household here? If you are, you will find fault with them in heaven. Your character is being tested and proved in this life, whether you will make a peaceable subject of God's kingdom in heaven. . . .

Summer after summer line upon line, testimony after testimony, has come from heaven to you, and the Word, the precious Word of God—and yet, where is your reform? Where is the cleansing of the soul temple? Where is the fitting up for the finishing touch of immortality? What are you doing? Have

you that faith that works, or have you that faith which does not
do anything for you?[1]

Sermons like this (and this is only a small slice of one great sermon)
would give people today hope in tough times as well as the assurance
of salvation. But it is typical Ellen White! How much more simple and
direct could she be?—"If you are right with God today, you are ready if
Christ should come today."

In other words, if someone should ask you, "If probation closed
today, would you be saved?" the answer should be, "Yes, I am God's
child. I am in His hand, and I am in a saving relationship with Him
today."

However, the real question for all of us is this: How can I remain in
a saving relationship with God?

In many ways, we find our answers in the Bible and in the writings
of Ellen White. In her book, *The Ministry of Healing,* she wrote:

> Nothing is apparently more helpless, yet really more invin-
> cible, than the soul that feels its nothingness and relies wholly
> on the merits of the Savior. By prayer, by the study of His
> word, by faith in His abiding presence, the weakest of human
> beings may live in contact with the living Christ, and He will
> hold them by a hand that will never let go.[2]

What a promise! She gives three very simple steps in maintaining
present assurance, and not one requires a college education: (1) prayer,
(2) Bible study, and (3) faith in God's abiding presence. He pledges His
honor, He stakes the integrity of the universe on this promise—that
those who sincerely, even tearfully, follow this simple formula will never
be snatched out of His hand. Why? Because He will never let go!

After this counsel, Ellen White introduced several Bible texts:

> These precious words every soul that abides in Christ may
> make his own. He may say:
>
> "I will look unto the Lord;
> I will wait for the God of my salvation:
> My God will hear me.
> Rejoice not against me, O mine enemy:
> When I fall, I shall arise;
> When I sit in darkness,
> The Lord shall be a light unto me." Micah 7:7, 8.

"He will again have compassion on us,
He will blot out our iniquities;
Yea, Thou wilt cast all our sins into the depths of the sea!"
Micah 7:19, Noyes.

God has promised:

"I will make a man more precious than fine gold;
Even a man than the golden wedge of Ophir." Isaiah 13:12.

"Though ye have lain among the pots,
Yet shall ye be as the wings of a dove covered with silver,
And her feathers with yellow gold." Psalm 68:13.

Those whom Christ has forgiven most will love Him most. These are they who in the final day will stand nearest to His throne. "They shall see His face; and His name shall be in their foreheads." Revelation 22:4.[3]

First step—prayer

Wonderful, powerful promises! Now, let's look again at the three-fold formula for maintaining present salvation. Prayer is such an obvious suggestion—why does it seem so hard at times? If prayer is opening the heart to God as to a friend,[4] why do we find it so difficult? Yes, we all have gone through those dark moments when the hellish shadow of Satan eclipses the noonday sun.

But God also knows all this! He knows exactly what is happening within our minds, so distracted by our worries and troubles. And you can be sure that the light of the Holy Spirit is trying to break through this darkness, this fog that seems to paralyze spiritual thoughts.

I think the first step in opening up our prayer life is to go back to the basics:

- We are weak human beings, full of regrets and guilt (Psalm 51:2, 3).
- God did not send Jesus to fellowship with those who have never made mistakes; He came to rescue sinners like you and me (Mark 2:17).
- None of us has gone so far that Jesus cannot find us, even to save "to the uttermost" (Hebrews 7:25).
- Jesus promised that " 'the one who comes to Me I will by no means cast out' " (John 6:37).
- The key word is "come"!

Nowhere in the Bible are we to "do something" before God will hear us. Always, it is "come"—" 'Come to Me, all you who labor and are heavy laden' " (Matthew 11:28). "The Spirit and the bride say, 'Come' " (Revelation 22:17). Nowhere in the Bible are we told to go to Mecca, the religious capital of Saudi Arabia, making a *hadj* (pilgrimage) which is one of the five duties of a Moslem. Or to go to Rome to ascend Pilate's staircase on our knees for a special indulgence. Or even to go to our own church! We are "to come" to the realization that God is no farther away than our own hands and feet, no further than the cries in our hearts! He hears every sob! Every frustration! Every hurt!

We must remember that prayer does not tell God something that He does not know; it is letting God tell us something we do not know or remember.[5]

But what shall we pray about? *Please, Lord, remove the shadows that seem to hide You. I need peace, I need the strength of Your everlasting arms to lean on. Shake up all the murky thoughts in my mind so that everything takes on Your perspective. Strengthen my decision to put You first in my thoughts and my plans. Sink deeply into my soul the knowledge that You are "too wise to err, and too good to withhold any good thing from them that walk uprightly."[6]*

We must keep Jesus in the forefront of our thoughts, hour by hour. We remember that He came for one primary purpose—to tell the truth about God. That He was representing God. That He came as every child comes into this world, not as a divine prince with special prerogatives, but with all the liabilities and weaknesses that every child is burdened with at birth.[7] That He, too, had dark, cloudy days "when He offered up prayers and supplications with vehement cries and tears" (Hebrews 5:7). That He was "tempted as we are yet without sin" (Hebrews 4:15). That, "in all things, He had to be made like His brethren, that He might be a merciful and faithful High Priest . . . for in that He Himself has suffered being tempted, He is able to aid those who are tempted" (Hebrews 2:17, 18).

In other words, Jesus went through every trial, every insult, every frazzlement, every disappointment that we experience so that He could give us the confidence that He truly has something to say to us during our dark days. Prayer is a matter of getting all this straightened out in our minds.

Second step—Bible study

The next step in maintaining our saving relationship with Jesus is Bible study. A saving relationship means that we are right every day with God, that every day we are certain that if we should die today, we are saved.

Where does one begin to find the light and peace that seem so far away at times? I can only tell you what has worked for me. On different occasions, I have set aside an hour to read Mark's Gospel. Pithy, forceful, direct—the story of Jesus comes through like a fleet of F-22 Raptors. Or, when perplexed, I have told God that I would not put down the book of Proverbs until I got my answer. Sometimes it comes by the fourth chapter. Sometimes much further. But always the answer has come. Sometimes I read the Psalms, especially Psalms 22, 23, 27, 31, 33, 37, 39, 51, etc.

More often than not, I read the Gospel of John, especially focusing on the words of Jesus. Just let the words of Jesus sink in as if you are on the mountainside or in the boat, listening to Him as if you were one of the disciples. There is power in the words of Jesus. Power in the written Word!

If you would like a fresh approach, read the *Good News Bible.* It is as reliable as most any other translation. In this Bible, read Philippians in one sitting; it won't take long.

Many years ago a passage in *The Desire of Ages,* made a profound impression on me. Perhaps it has meant much to you as well:

> The life of Christ that gives life to the world is in His word. It was by His word that Jesus healed disease and cast out demons; by His word He stilled the sea, and raised the dead; and the people bore witness that His word was with power. He spoke the word of God, as He had spoken through all the prophets and teachers of the Old Testament. The whole Bible is a manifestation of Christ, and the Savior desired to fix the faith of His followers on the word. When His visible presence should be withdrawn, the word must be their source of power. Like their Master, they were to live "by every word that proceedeth out of the mouth of God." Matt. 4:4.[8]

I freely admit that I have an addiction. Some call it "food"! I have craved it for years! Norma and I enjoy a great buffet. We can tell you some of the best from Hawaii to Florida, although we used to get more for our money when we were younger!

Every morning Norma fixes the same breakfast (I mean the *same* breakfast *every* morning) except Sunday. Every day we smother our tablespoon of ground flax seed with Weimar Institute granola, date nuggets, raisins, banana, and soy milk, plus an orange. It is the only kind of breakfast that keeps us for five hours! We look forward to breakfast; it has become one of our favorite friends!

You are wondering about Sunday. Ah! We each eat a full twelve-minute waffle made of two cups of oats, three cups of water, one-third cup of raw cashews or almonds, two tablespoons of whole-wheat flour, and a half teaspoon of salt! Of course, the topping—almond butter lavishly spread and drowned by a date-orange juice compote, and a mix of strawberries, blueberries, and other fruit available. Are we addicted? You bet!

Why do I tell you all this? Just as our physical food provides us with so much enjoyment, so does the Word. If fact, it is more than enjoyment; we can't function long without a good breakfast. Our breakfasts sustain us just as the Word of God sustains us. If emergencies come up, I soon sense I am not doing well without a good breakfast. So it is when I try to slide through the busy day without an adequate intake from the Word.

How many days do you think I can go without eating properly? Not many! I find myself becoming short with my answers, troubled over little things, and not very upbeat. This is an exact parallel to the days when life seems so frazzled that I begin to slide through meaningful devotional time. Maybe I can't recite to you exactly what I read last week for my Bible study any more than I can remember what I ate for lunch last Wednesday. But I do know that what I ate for lunch nourished me and made me a better person. And I know that what I read and digested in my devotional time last Wednesday also nourished me. I know you get my point.

There is something else I learned years ago: Knowing what theologians have said about the Bible doesn't feed me—although I am a trained theologian with three graduate degrees. I can sound educated, just quoting what others have written about God, the universe, or the Bible. But, frankly, all that sometimes gives me only a headache as I try to balance all their contradictions.

Then it dawned on me. There is something vastly more important than sounding well-read. Something more important than making sure I had hundreds of footnotes of what contemporary theologians have said on the subject. Something more important than being current on what others have said about the Bible, as good as their insights may be. That something else was understanding for myself why all the churches and their divisions through the centuries can't agree on the gospel and on the meaning of faith and grace! So I looked at the Bible and the writings of Ellen White in a new way, no longer hemmed in by conventional theologies. I began to see the big picture as never before; we call it the "Great Controversy Theme." This theme tells us not merely that there is a cosmic war going on between God and

Satan and that God wins. It tells us *why* the controversy began in the first place and how it must be settled so that rebellion will never arise again. For me, these concepts unfolded a fresh way of looking at the gospel and the biblical meaning of faith and grace that has kept Christianity divided so many years.

My purpose in saying this is simply to point to the obvious—we must eat breakfast for ourselves. No one can eat my breakfast for me. Or, for you! In the same way, we must "eat" what God's messengers have said through the years for ourselves—and not primarily through the eyes and pen of someone else. There is not much sense complaining about being spiritually hungry when we stay away from where the food is.

I like the way Ellen White put it:

> As we must eat for ourselves in order to receive nourishment, so we must receive the word for ourselves. We are not to obtain it merely through the medium of another's mind. We should carefully study the Bible, asking God for the aid of the Holy Spirit, that we may understand His word. We should take one verse, and concentrate the mind on the task of ascertaining the thought which God has put in that verse for us. We should dwell upon the thought until it becomes our own, and we know "what saith the Lord."[9]

To put it another way, in order to "grow up" spiritually, we must eat from the Word ourselves. We must make the experiences related in God's word, our experiences. Prayer and promise, precept and warning, are ours. This is what John meant by "abiding in Christ" as a branch "abides" in the main vine. This is the faith experience that sometimes sounds so mystical. And shouldn't be!

Again, Ellen White nailed it to the wall of my understanding:

> As faith thus receives and assimilates the principles of truth, they become a part of the being and the motive power of the life. The word of God, received into the soul, molds the thoughts, and enters into the development of character.[10]

This is how Jesus Himself grew "in wisdom and stature, and in favor with God and men" (Luke 2:52). "Since He gained knowledge as we may do, His intimate acquaintance with the Scriptures shows how diligently His early years were given to the study of God's word."[11]

I feel that I must linger on these thoughts because they have been so precious to me for many years. There is no mystery to spiritual growth, no mystery to a saving relationship with Jesus. The formula is so easy that even children may understand—but so difficult for the proud heart that thinks only profound theological reasoning can produce heart certainty or even mind certainty. Let these words sing to your soul:

> As they feed upon His word, they find that it is spirit and life. The word destroys the natural, earthly nature, and imparts a new life in Christ Jesus. The Holy Spirit comes to the soul as a Comforter. By the transforming agency of His grace, the image of God is reproduced in the disciple; he becomes a new creature. Love takes the place of hatred, and the heart receives the divine similitude. This is what it means to live "by every word that proceedeth out of the mouth of God." This is eating the Bread that comes down from heaven.[12]

Third step—faith that abides

Now to the third part of the formula, "faith in His abiding presence," by which "the weakest of human beings may live in contact with the living Christ, [whereby] He will hold them by a hand that will never let go."[13]

The key word here is *faith*—the word that has troubled Christians for centuries. Misunderstanding this word has caused every division within Christianity since apostolic days. In the next chapter we will examine the meaning of this word so that you will never doubt again as to how you should have "full assurance of faith" (Hebrews 10:22) *now!*

But for now I can't emphasize enough that a powerful sense of our Lord's "abiding presence" is one of the three lines of defense against Satan's wiles that we have been working out in our formula. Too often we think of Satan's temptations as coming from the outside, from the entertainment world, for example, or from associates without Christian goals or from hobbies that take up too much precious time, etc. I know those areas are fairly easy to spot and avoid as God helps us to make our choices a lifelong habit.

But the more subtle temptations that are determining the future, hour by hour, are those sticky areas such as self-importance, self-indulgence, pretense, inappropriate control over others, self-justification, etc. These are areas that are not often seen by others because we are good at covering them up, good at pretense. External bad habits we can eliminate fairly quickly in order to remain "good and regular" members of the church. But these more unseen weaknesses of the flesh are by far the most damaging to spiritual growth.

I think often—primarily for my own reflection because I need these words as much as anyone reading these pages—of those yellow flags and red lights in passages such as the following:

> You are just as dependent upon Christ, in order to live a holy life, as is the branch upon the parent stock for growth and fruitfulness. Apart from Him you have no life. You have no power to resist temptation or to grow in grace and holiness. Abiding in Him, you may flourish. Drawing your life from Him, you will not wither nor be fruitless.[14]

"Abiding in Him" is more than a nice motto. It is the open secret to consistent honesty, kindness, graciousness, gentleness, and compassion for others. No matter how much willpower the strongest-minded man or woman may have, without "abiding in Him" those moments come when all the willpower in the world does not hold back the curt word, the hard tone, the indiscreet touch and more.

Some ask, "How do I abide, and keep up a prayer life and Bible study?" And Ellen White answers:

> In the same way as you received Him at first, "As ye have therefore received Christ Jesus the Lord, so walk ye in Him" (Colossians 2:6). . . . You gave yourself to God, to be His wholly, to serve and obey Him, and you took Christ as your Savior. You could not yourself atone for your sins or change your heart; but having given yourself to God, you believe that He for Christ's sake did all this for you. By *faith* you became Christ's, and by faith you are to grow up in Him—by giving and taking. You are to *give* all—your heart, your will, your service—give yourself to Him to obey all His requirements; and you must *take* all—Christ, the fullness of all blessing, to abide in your heart, to be your strength, your righteousness, your everlasting helper—to give you power to obey.[15]

This kind of counsel should not be read hurriedly. I guarantee you did not get the impact of that paragraph in your first reading. I still need to take one sentence at a time, and I have read that page probably fifty times!

Here is what these insights have meant to me:

• We emphasize "you are to give all," but sail over "you must *take* all."

- We emphasize "you are to give all" because we realize our part in the divine-human co-op plan (see Philippians 2:12). "Give all" means absolute surrender of whatever habit, possession, or practice the light of the Holy Spirit focuses on (see Proverbs 3:5-8; Matthew 16:24).
- We often don't ponder the promise in "you must *take* all." Without drinking in all that this promise implies, our Christian path becomes more duty than pleasure where self-denial becomes a cloud over the joy of salvation. We grit our teeth to make sure that we have surrendered *all*.
- Pause for a moment and bask in this promise: Jesus, our Lord and High Priest, is promising to abide in us, to think His thoughts through our thoughts, to enable us to love others as He loved others, to live out through us the way that He met temptations of all kinds (see Galatians 2:20). That is, "take all" that he wants to work out in our lives (see Philippians 2:13)—whatever it takes to help us obey His wisdom.
- But "take all" means far more than merely asking Him to fulfill His promises by living within us. Asking and taking are light years apart! The real connection begins when we accept His promise *already given to us* to be—in us—our thoughts, our energy, our moral clarity. We "take all" that He has promised to be for us, working out "both to will and to do for His good pleasure" (Philippians 2:13).
- The core of our daily prayers is no longer "asking" but rather "thanking" Him for His promise to live within us so that our "willing and doing" is approximating what He willed and did while here on earth.
- This constant awareness through the day and night is the bedrock of our assurance of faith. This is the way faith works! The question of whether you are in a saved relationship with Jesus doesn't arise any more than a son wonders if the woman in the home who feeds and clothes him is his mother! It seems so natural for a son to thank his mother for loving him and caring for him in the days to come! The son keeps abiding in his mother's love, never doubting that love any more than he doubts that the sun will shine tomorrow. That is genuine assurance!
- "Taking all" that Jesus wants to give us radically reduces our fears. All through the day we are making a habit of saying, "Lord Jesus, I have given You my will. Thank You for living out Your victory in me." It's His promise—He will live out His desires and His responses to temptation in us even as He did two thousand years

ago! We talk this confidence until it becomes a chorus that we hum
night and day.

And then Ellen White continues with a paragraph that hundreds
of thousands have pasted on their refrigerators or their bathroom
mirrors:

> Consecrate yourself to God in the morning; make this your
> very first work. Let your prayer be, "Take me, O Lord, as wholly
> Thine. I lay all my plans at Thy feet. Use me today in Thy
> service. Abide with me, and let all my work be wrought in
> Thee." This is a daily matter. Each morning consecrate your-
> self to God for that day. Surrender all your plans to Him, to be
> carried out or given up as His providence shall indicate. Thus
> day by day you may be giving your life into the hands of God,
> and thus your life will be molded more and more after the life
> of Christ.[16]

It seems that the word *abide* carries with it an assortment of other
thoughts to remember daily. *Abide* suggests rest, but also stability, and
confidence. When Jesus told us " 'Come to Me . . . and I will give you
rest,' " He didn't mean inactivity. He meant what *abide* means—the place
where you can find a safe place to build your life. Jesus went on, " 'Take
my yoke upon you. . . . For My yoke is easy and My burden is light' "
(Matthew 11:28-30). Christians who have found their "abiding place,"
find renewed energy to take on the day, to reach out to others who
need help, to lean into the future, learning new ideas and new ways to
be truly useful in their church activities.

Our challenge is to keep ourselves "abiding in Him" for Satan has
a thousand distractions, many of which are arguably good in themselves. But even good things can be the enemy of the best. On top of
all the "good" things that drown out the "best," we have the unrelent-
ing tug of the world, its pleasures and its cares, its perplexities, sorrows, and disappointments. Even our own faults may shut out the
light and turn off the voice of the Spirit.

The secret of abiding is realizing that even when we drift (as we
often do) we still know where peace, rest, and confidence really are.
Go back to where you left Him.

> Put away all doubt; dismiss your fears. Say with the apostle
> Paul, "I live; yet not I, but Christ liveth in me: and the life which
> I now live in the flesh I live by the faith of the Son of God, who

loved me, and gave Himself for me" Galatians 2:20. Rest in God. He is able to keep that which you have committed to Him. If you will leave yourself in His hands, He will bring you off more than conqueror through Him that has loved you.[17]

Another secret of abiding in Christ is not to be "overly righteous" (Ecclesiastes 7:16). I know that may sound strange at first. But some people are extremely conscientious to the extent that they "dwell upon their own faults and weaknesses."[18] It becomes almost pathological. In fact, focusing inordinately on "assurance" and "being saved" could be an egocentric concern. I like Ellen White's counsel on this point:

> We should not make self the center and indulge anxiety and fear as to whether we shall be saved. All this turns the soul away from the Source of our strength. Commit the keeping of your soul to God, and trust in Him. Talk and think of Jesus. Let self be lost in Him. Put away all doubt; dismiss your fears. Say with the apostle Paul, "I live; yet not I, but Christ liveth in me: and the life which I now live in the flesh I live by the faith of the Son of God, who loved me, and gave Himself for me." Galatians 2:20. Rest in God. He is able to keep that which you have committed to Him.[19]

One caution: A consistent devotional life is not only a private affair. Prayer, study, and faith are the components of maturing Christians who are becoming better parents, grandparents, spouses, teachers, preachers, administrators, students, and more devoted sons and daughters. In all of our devotions, we must daily tell our heavenly Father that we *choose* to be His loyal followers. This is more than a wish or a desire—it is choosing to be loyal in whatever comes up that day. Without that daily choosing, our devotional habits can easily become false security—a "righteousness by devotions" work track.

This is the formula for maintaining genuine assurance: prayer, study, faith, daily choosing, daily asking for help from our heavenly Father to transform our choices into life habits of loving service to others.

Before going on, I must keep assuring you that no one I know has made a straight line to spiritual maturity. All of us are stumbling along. But we must keep stumbling forward. God is good at picking us up. That's what fathers do very well. And God is our heavenly Father. So keep moving on!

In a later chapter, we will look at how habits are formed. God is helping us grow up (Ephesians 4:13) so that we can be truly depended on in all situations to say "Yes" to Him and "No" to sin.[20] And that will be a continual learning experience until we reach that point the whole universe is waiting for—when God's people "are sealed in their foreheads. It is not any seal or mark that can be seen, but a settling into the truth, both intellectually and spiritually, so they cannot be moved."[21]

That "settling into the truth" describes those who have been permitting the Holy Spirit to empower them, by gentle guidance and direct energy, with those "settled" neural patterns wherein they can be counted on to be faithful witnesses to the power of the gospel (see Romans 1:16). They truly will be safe to save because in them rebellion will not arise a second time (see Nahum 1:9). They will never be moved in their loyalty to God, never ever be an embarrassment to Him as long as eternity lasts!

I know some are thinking, like "This sounds too much for me! I don't have that much faith!" In our next chapter, let's think about how much faith we need to have genuine assurance. When we get this word, "faith," right, many worries will vanish! Read on.

---

[1] *Sermons and Talks*, vol. 1, pp. 202–204, emphasis supplied.

[2] Page 182.

[3] Ibid., p. 182.

[4] See Ellen G. White, *Steps to Christ*, p. 93.

[5] See p. 93.

[6] *Steps to Christ*, p. 96.

[7] See Ellen G. White, *The Desire of Ages*, p. 49.

[8] Page 390.

[9] Ibid.

[10] Ibid.

[11] Ibid., p. 70.

[12] Ibid., p. 391.

[13] Ellen G. White, *The Ministry of Healing*, p. 182.

[14] Ellen G. White, *Steps to Christ*, p. 69.

[15] Ibid., pp. 69, 70.

[16] Ibid., p. 70.

[17] Ibid., p. 72

[18] Ibid., p. 71.

[19] Ibid., p. 72.

[20] "For the grace of God that brings salvation has appeared to all men. It teaches us to say 'No' to ungodliness and worldly passions, and to live self-controlled, upright, and godly lives in this present age, while we wait for the blessed hope—the glorious appearing of our great God and Savior, Jesus Christ, who gave himself for us to redeem us from all wickedness and to purify for himself a people that are his very own, eager to do what is good" (Titus 2:11-14, NIV).

[21] Ellen G. White, *Last Day Events*, pp. 219, 220.

CHAPTER EIGHT

How Much Faith Must I Have?

"Let us draw near with a true heart in full assurance of faith, having our hearts sprinkled from an evil conscience. . . . Let us hold fast the confession of our hope without wavering, for He who promised is faithful" (Hebrews 10:22, 23).

We have referred to this verse in previous chapters. Precious, isn't it! Several important principles are emphasized in this verse:

- Full assurance depends on our faith; assurance is not something else in addition to faith.
- Full assurance of faith cleanses the conscience of guilt, despair, and sinful thoughts.
- The basis for hope is not our faith, but God's faithfulness.
- The basis for faith is not in our feelings or our reasoning, but in God's faithfulness.

Although many Christians have memorized this text, Christianity for centuries has been terribly divided over what this text means. The problem lies in how "faith" is defined. How we understand the meaning of faith determines the meaning of assurance.

The same problem arises when we use the phrase, "righteousness by faith." Again, in order to understand what "righteousness by faith," means, we must get the meaning of "faith" right.

In fact, when we get the meaning of faith right, all other biblical doctrines quickly make sense and add to the Christian's assurance. Why? Because when we get faith right, we are also getting the character of God right—and that makes all the difference in understanding the Bible.

So what is faith? It is more than hearing the right words. Many spouses hear these words, "I love you," with all the embellishments, but they still go through the years, not sure. Why? Because their mates are not always where they should be; their late-night excuses don't seem to add up, etc.

What is going on here? All these spouses are hearing the right words; they are even being told the right words. So what is wrong? Those words are not being responded to with the "assurance of faith." I can't keep telling my wife, "All you need to do is believe!" Obviously, a spouse needs more than words to build faith.

But that brings us to another problem, for isn't that what the Bible tells us to do—"Believe on the Lord Jesus Christ and thou shalt be saved" (Acts 16:31, KJV)? And did not the Jews fail, because they did not "believe"? And so the problem builds.

New Testament faith is more than

- believing in Jesus in the same way as we believe that the earth is 93 million miles away from the sun;
- a blind leap in the dark when all else fails;
- a denominational belief, such as the Methodist "faith" or the Adventist "faith";
- "keeping the faith, baby" —the slogan of the '60s and '70s equating faith with deep loyalties;
- confidence in the scientific process and medical research;
- trusting the surgeon who promises to excise your brain tumor.

Just for further clarification, try inserting any of the above definitions of faith that we commonly use every day in the English language into the formula, "righteousness by faith," or "assurance of faith." You may try, but they won't work. Why? Because in the New Testament, "faith" has a distinctive meaning, and only the New Testament can help us understand that meaning.

The problem with the word *faith* is that many English Bibles translate the Greek infinitive, *pisteuo*, as "to believe," but its noun form, *pistis*, is translated as "faith."[1] What is going on? The simple answer is that we don't have a verb in English that says, "to faith." We say that the swimmer swims, the writer writes, the fearful fear, but we can't (or won't) say in English, the faithful "faiths."

French has the same problem: *foi* (noun) and *croire* (verb); Latin: *fides* (noun) and *credere* (verb). Why does this problem exist? Because language does not develop willy-nilly. In the early Christian church, faith, unfortunately, became a matter of believing biblical information, and so a man of faith was a man who believed in certain doctrines. And that is why we have so many deep divisions within Christianity, so many contradictory atonement theories.

But the Germans do not have this problem—they have another one that is even more damaging. It's true that Germans do not separate the noun for faith (*Glaube*) from the verb (*Glauben*). The German religious mind, largely influenced by Luther's translation of the Bible, has no trouble linguistically in joining the noun, *Glaube,* and the verb, *Glauben.* The huge problem lies in the fact that they define *Glaube* and *Glauben* as "belief" or "to believe" as one would believe in the law of gravity. I remember teaching a Sabbath School class in North Dakota with mostly Germans in the class. To make my point regarding the meaning of faith, I asked them to say, "I have faith in Jesus" (*"Ich glaube an Jesus"*). Then I asked them to say, "I believe you have blue eyes" (*"Ich glaube . . ."*)—then they caught themselves. Several tried, but one finally said, "Either we have no word for 'believe,' or we have no word for 'faith.' " And that has been the German problem since Luther translated the Bible into German in the sixteenth century.

I am going over all this to show that understanding the word "faith" in the New Testament is not as easy as some have made it out to be. In fact, almost any Christian church assumes that all other Christian churches define faith as it does. Wrong!

This language problem has deeply affected modern theology. After reading this far, you can see the problem immediately when someone insists that "all you have to do is believe on the Lord Jesus Christ, and you are saved." But you may still be unsure as to how to respond.

For example, when Paul and Silas told the jailor what to do to be saved, the English translations usually say, " 'Believe on the Lord Jesus Christ, and you will be saved' " (Acts 16:31). But what Paul really said was: "Have faith in the Lord Jesus Christ, and you will be saved." In other words, "Mr. Jailer, I don't want you to merely believe that Jesus died on the cross and that He promised forgiveness for all your sins. I want you to make Him your Lord, and I want you to have faith in Him—trusting, obedient faith—and to be His loyal follower like I am." (After all, many people in that day believed that Jesus died on the cross, but they did not have faith!)

This may sound somewhat heavy, but I assure you that getting a correct definition of faith will have everything to do with your sense of assurance—that is, your saving relationship with Jesus today. Further, faith is one of the key characteristics of those who are prepared for Jesus to come, separating them from many other "believers" in the end time who will hear the Lord's awful pronouncement, "I never knew you for what you said you were."

In other words, we better get the meaning of faith right! Why? Because understanding how to find the "assurance of faith" is at the top of the list!

We are going to see that faith is more than agreement with facts, even facts about Jesus. It is more than mental conviction, more than a passive acceptance of God's work for us. Furthermore, error does not become truth merely because a person has faith in it. Faith in error will not produce the fruit of truth no matter how sincere a person may be. Ellen White saw all this clearly:

> Faith is the medium through which truth or error finds a lodging place in the mind. It is by the same act of mind that truth or error is received, but it makes a decided difference whether we believe the Word of God or the sayings of men. When Christ revealed Himself to Paul, and he was convinced that he was persecuting Jesus in the person of His saints, he accepted the truth as it is in Jesus. A transforming power was manifested on mind and character, and he became a new man in Christ Jesus. He received the truth so fully that neither earth nor hell could shake his faith.[2]

New Testament faith is specific and unique. It describes Christians who appreciate what Jesus has done for them and who then choose to believe, trust, and obey Him. Getting the mission and message of Jesus right will give us a true definition of faith—and a true definition of faith will give us the correct view of why Jesus came and died and what He wants us to do about it.

Paul knew that his first-century hearers needed a clear understanding of faith. After giving his well-known definition in Hebrews 11:1—"Faith is being sure of what we hope for and certain of what we do not see" (NIV)—he realized that a cold definition was not enough. So he hastened to write a long chapter that has become a classic in world literature. He pictured faith in three dimensions, in living color. "By faith," we learn that:

- Men of old received divine approval.
- Abel offered to God a more acceptable sacrifice.
- Enoch was taken up so that he should not see death.
- Noah constructed an ark.

- Abraham obeyed and went out, not knowing where he was to go.
- Sarah herself received power to conceive.
- Moses, when he was born, was hid for three months by his parents.
- Moses, when he was grown up, refused to be called the son of Pharaoh's daughter.
- Moses esteemed Christ greater riches than the treasures of Egypt.
- The people passed through the Red Sea.
- The walls of Jericho fell down.
- Men and women conquered kingdoms, enforced justice, received promises, stopped the mouths of lions, quenched raging fire, escaped the edge of the sword, became mighty in war, put foreign armies to flight.

Such men and women were uncommon heroes of their generation. They did not fade into the wallpaper or blend into the spirit of their age. They did not live their lives in a corner, off the beaten path, in order to quietly read their Bibles and say their prayers.

Although it is easy to remember them for their remarkable achievements, we must never forget that it was their faith that made them the individual that we honor. When we review the results of the faith that God approves, it is obvious that faith is more than a blind leap in the dark, more than mere mental belief, even more than enthusiasm and zeal.

For biblical men and women, faith was the way—the only right way—for each of them to relate to God. It involved (1) an appreciation for what God had done for them; (2) a correct understanding of God's plan for them; (3) the will to respond as He wanted; and (4) an abiding trust that He would continue to do His part if they would do theirs.

For all these biblical heroes, in both Old and New Testaments, faith was saying "Yes" to God, to whatever He commanded. Faith was appreciation, belief, trust, obedience, and deepest assurance all wrapped up in a cheerful companionship with their Lord and Master.

In other words, faith involves the intellect, the will, and commitment—but it is none of these in themselves. Faith is simply the whole person saying "Yes" to God, knowing by objective evidence and personal experience (remember John's testimony in 1 John 1:1-4) that there is nothing deceptive, unreal, or empty about what God has said or what faith has experienced.[3]

All this is reflected in Peter's experience at Caesarea Phillipi, recorded in Matthew 16:13-20. Faith is what happened to Peter on that memorable occasion.

Remember our Lord's question to His disciples: " 'But who do you say that I am?' " (verse 15). Our Lord's questions came at a decisive hour in His ministry. He and the Twelve had just left Galilee after many pressing days of teaching, healing, and conflict with hostile church leaders who harassed them at every turn. But Jesus was now alone with His closest friends on earth, and He knew that time was running out.

If anyone would carry on His mission, such would have to come from this small group. Soon they would be the only visible link between God's plan of salvation and a lost world who had to hear it. Did they really know who Jesus was? Did they understand why He came and why He had to die? Were they convinced that Jesus was more than a great Teacher sent from God? Would their conviction be persuasive and convincing to others who would not even have seen Jesus? After all, men and women who knew their Scriptures (Old Testament), men and women who did listen to Jesus and did see His miracles, were having difficulty accepting Him for whom He said He was.

In such circumstances, Jesus put the question: " 'But who do you say that I am?' " (verse 15).

Why didn't Jesus boldly tell them who He was, why He came, and why He was soon to be murdered? Isn't that the most important information that human beings should know (see John 17:3)?

The fact that Jesus does not Himself declare His status leads us straight into the heart of the gospel and the meaning of faith. Why does Jesus ask a question rather than just tell them the answer? Because biblical faith does not come at the end of a theological lecture nor even at the end of a good Bible study! It is not something worked out in the head alone. If that were so, then those who do not have a theological degree would not have much chance of understanding the gospel!

Let's say this in a different way. Just to know about the historical Jesus—how He was born, what He did for thirty-three years, when and how He died, the fact of His resurrection—may make a person doctrinally orthodox. But all that knowledge is not yet faith! Judas knew all that as well as Peter! That is why Jesus asked His question.

And that is why, after Peter said, " 'You are the Christ [Messiah], the Son of the living God' " (verse 16), Jesus could say, " 'Blessed are you, Simon Bar-Jonah, for flesh and blood has not revealed this to you, but My Father who is in heaven' " (verse 17).

What did Jesus mean? Jesus was recognizing that Peter was responding to more than historical information. After all, the religious leaders of the day and the thousands of people who saw His miracles and heard His messages had all the facts that Peter had—and they crucified Jesus.

But Peter was responding to the inner word of the Holy Spirit who had been working on his heart. The inner word was being constantly reaffirmed by the living Word, and vice versa. Everything Jesus said about Peter's own secret life was hitting the mark. Peter knew that he was face to face with God Himself. Peter called Jesus "Lord," not because he had more information than anyone else, but because he was willing to commit his life to his Lord. He was a struggling rebel who capitulated. He had lots of growing yet to do, but that moment had come when he called his Teacher, his "Lord."

Jesus probably went on: "Peter, you understand what I have been trying to do. You now see that it would have been impossible to proclaim Myself as God—what more evidence could I have given? All I can do is reveal Myself as the truth, and explain why I do what I do, and wait—wait for you to see and believe and trust and commit! I must wait until faith is born!"

In Christ's reply we can see the inner process of true faith. Everyone, in some measure (see John 1:9; Romans 2:14-16) has heard the voice of the "Father who is in heaven." But not everyone responds to that voice as Peter did. Not everyone sees himself as a guilty, self-centered rebel in need of forgiveness and power.

The knowledge of faith is more than the good news learned about God. Faith also learns the truth about humankind. In the act of faith, when we call God, "Lord," at the same time we recognize ourselves as rebels who have insisted on our own way. In fact, no one truly believes he or she is lost, a rebel in need of help, without simultaneously saying "Yes" to God and falling at His feet for pardon and power.

For Peter it was decision time. He was ready to merge the voice within with the voice without—the Spirit affirming everything that Jesus was saying and doing. Peter's response was that of a rebel capitulating; it was the birth of faith. He knew that God had invaded his life and that God was telling the truth about him. Further, he knew that all his excuses for his self-centeredness were really cover-ups for sin and that faith was the opposite of sin. "The Master was right," Peter said to himself. "Everything He said about me is true and everything He said about Himself was exactly what my heart needed."

We find Jesus today in the same way that Peter discovered God in Jesus. Friendship with Jesus is one thing; faith in Jesus is another. Jesus had many friends who marveled at His messages. On Sunday they wanted to make Him "King of Israel" (see John 12:12-15). On Friday they wanted to crucify Him! What happened? The multitude was comfortable with Jesus when He seemed to be going their way. But when He exposed their insincerity, their unwillingness to make Him Lord, they tried to quiet their consciences by murdering Him. So it is today!

When Peter submitted to Jesus as Lord, he was telling the universe that he would trust and serve Jesus forever. His assurance of faith rested on his heart, prompted by the Spirit, saying "Amen" to his head that had come face to face with Jesus Christ.

Jesus went on to say: " 'You are Peter [a pebble], and on this rock [your confession] I will build my church, and the gates of Hades shall not prevail against it' " (Matthew 16:18). What could this mean?[4]

What, or who is the rock? Jesus is giving the simple formula for how faith is born and maintained. The foundation of the Christian's faith is his or her personal relationship with Jesus of Nazareth, the Rock of faith. I like the way Ellen White describes the birth of faith:

> Peter had expressed the truth which is the foundation of the church's faith. . . . There was only a handful of believers, against whom all the power of demons and evil men would be directed; yet the followers of Christ were not to fear. Built upon the Rock of their strength, they could not be overthrown. . . . Peter had expressed the truth which is the foundation of the church's faith, and Jesus now honored him as the representative of the whole body of believers. . . . The Rock of faith is the living presence of Christ in the church. Upon this the weakest may depend, and those who think themselves the strongest will prove to be the weakest, unless they make Christ their efficiency.[5]

The rock of faith must be a personal rock. Another's experience will not do, even as someone else cannot eat breakfast for us. The faith that keeps its balance when the storms roll in and everything on earth seems to shake is nothing that someone else can borrow. The oil that the foolish bridesmaids tried to borrow (see Matthew 25) was the faith of their companions. They learned to their sorrow that one must build his or her own faith just as one must do his own breathing.

Such faith is more than an intellectual experience, more than an emotional high. Faith changes the whole person—whatever he or she thinks, however he or she relates to another person or to God. In other words, faith is more than merely believing; it is a happening. Something far more than thinking and feeling occurs in faith. A new power, a new principle of life, takes over, and that person is a "new creation" (2 Corinthians 5:17).

That is why we have been saying, in different ways throughout this book, that biblical faith is more than simply "believing in Jesus." Who has described the experience of faith better than Ellen White?

> To talk of religion in a casual way, to pray without soul hunger and living faith, avails nothing. A nominal faith in Christ, which accepts Him merely as the Savior of the world, can never bring healing to the soul. The faith that is unto salvation is not a mere intellectual assent to the truth. He who waits for entire knowledge before he will exercise faith, cannot receive blessing from God. It is not enough to believe *about* Christ; we must believe *in* Him. The only faith that will benefit us is that which embraces Him as a personal Savior; which appropriates His merits to ourselves. Many hold faith as an opinion. Saving faith is a transaction by which those who receive Christ join themselves in covenant relation with God. Genuine faith is life. A living faith means an increase of vigor, a confiding trust, by which the soul becomes a conquering power.[6]

In other words, men and women of faith are converted rebels. Thinking and agreeing with God is not enough, nor is feeling enthusiastic and warm about His love for them sufficient. Merely telling the world that Jesus is God and Lord of the universe and that He has forgiven transgressors will not make men and women savable. Such information may be that of a scholar, but it does not make a man or woman of faith!

The biblical record describing men and women of faith takes us into the world of being and doing, not just looking through the windows of intellectual belief. Note this clear-cut description of living faith:

> It is not enough for us to believe that Jesus is not an impostor, and that the religion of the Bible is no cunningly devised fable. We may believe that the name of Jesus is the only name under heaven whereby man may be saved, and yet we may not through faith make Him our personal Savior. It is not enough to believe the theory of truth. It is not enough to make a profession of faith in Christ and have our names registered on the church roll. "He that keepeth His commandments dwelleth in Him, and He in him. And hereby we know that He abideth in us, by the Spirit which He hath given us." "Hereby we do know that we know Him if we keep His commandments." 1 John

3:24; 2:3. This is the genuine evidence of conversion. Whatever our profession, it amounts to nothing unless Christ is revealed in works of righteousness. The truth is to be planted in the heart. It is to control the mind and regulate the affections. The whole character must be stamped with the divine utterances. Every jot and tittle of the word of God is to be brought into the daily practice.[7]

Notice how Ellen White seamlessly joins the sense of "abiding," "obedience," and living "faith"—the themes of this book. Faith is built on the evidence and promises of what the Bible says about Jesus. But the "assurance of faith" rests on the person's decision to make Jesus Lord of his or her life. Thus, with John, we know that the Holy Spirit, the inner word, merges with the external Word, giving us the assurance that we are God's children.

How do I know all this? Because He told me so. Because I trust Him. And because it is true in my experience. And in yours! That sense of trusting Him who is faithful becomes the rock of our faith.

Why is all this so important? Because

- Living in faith is living as Jesus did, nurtured constantly by the Spirit.
- Living in faith develops the character of Jesus.
- Reflecting the character of Jesus is the aim of faith.
- The aim of faith is to prepare people in these end times to be a part of that group described in Revelation 14:12: "Here is the patience [endurance] of the saints; here are those who keep the commandments of God and the faith of Jesus."
- This kind of simple Bible logic is our firm foundation for the "assurance of faith" (Hebrews 10:22).

I know some are thinking: This sounds so one-sided! What about grace! How does this emphasis on faith relate to God's grace "that brings salvation . . . to all men" (Titus 2:11)? Let's talk about grace in our next chapter.

---

[1] For example: "But to him who does not work but believes on Him who justifies the ungodly, his faith is accounted for righteousness" (Romans 4:5). The verb *believes*, comes from the same root as does the noun *faith*, but one would never know it in English. This text is only one of many where the meaning is obscured by this disconnect in English between the noun and verb. The verse should be accurately translated, "but to him who does not work but has faith in Him who justifies the ungodly, his faith is accounted for righteousness."

[2] *Selected Messages,* book 1, p. 346.

[3] See Ellen G. White, *The Ministry of Healing,* p. 461.

[4] Unfortunately, Peter did not walk a straight path. He made Jesus his Lord, but he did not entirely realize what that meant. During that awful night when Peter denied his Lord three times, he revealed that in his headstrong honesty "he did not know himself. . . . The Savior saw in him a self-love and assurance that would overbear even his love for Christ" (Ellen G. White, *The Desire of Ages,* p. 673). Here is a clear example of presumptuous assurance in a man who thought he was loyal. Jesus wanted Peter to look deeper into his human weakness and to have deeper faith.

[5] *The Desire of Ages,* pp. 412–414.

[6] Ibid., p. 347.

[7] *Christ's Object Lessons,* pp. 312–314. In the same book she writes, "In all who will submit themselves to the Holy Spirit a new principle of life is to be implanted; the lost image of God is to be restored in humanity. . . . A profession of faith and the possession of truth in the soul are two different things. The mere knowledge of truth is not enough. We may possess this, but the tenor of our thoughts may not be changed. The heart must be converted and sanctified. . . . True obedience is the outworking of a principle within. It springs from the love of righteousness, the love of the law of God. The essence of all righteousness is loyalty to our Redeemer. This will lead us to do right because it is right—because right doing is pleasing to God" (Ibid., pp. 96–98).

CHAPTER NINE

How Grace Relates to Faith

We want to know how grace and faith relate to the "assurance of faith" (Hebrews 10:22). Let's make a quick overview first of how grace relates to faith itself.

Perhaps the clearest formula of salvation, the classic expression of how men and women are saved, is Paul's statement: "For by grace you have been saved through faith" (Ephesians 2:8). Here again, something that should be so simple has become the crux of controversy for centuries. Men and women have been tortured and killed because they disagreed with others over the meaning of this text!

What is the problem? As we have said before, the misunderstanding of what faith means has caused almost every division within Christianity to this moment.[1] We see the confusion highlighted when the Roman Catholic, the Calvinist Evangelical, the Lutheran, and the Wesleyan Methodist attempt to explain that text to each other!

Paul is not saying that salvation is the result of either grace alone or faith alone. Salvation is not all God's part, nor is it all man's. If it were by grace alone, it could not be by faith alone.

Paul is saying that faith is the condition that makes salvation possible. But faith is not the cause—grace is. Grace is God taking the initiative. God is the faithful Shepherd, looking for every lost sheep, and no sheep can ever say that he or she did not hear the voice of the Shepherd (see John 1:9; Romans 2:14-16). But grace is frustrated when faith is absent.

Grace is a facet of God's love (*agape*), and as it is generally used in the New Testament it describes whatever God has done, is doing, and will do to conform men and women "to the image of His Son" (Romans

8:29). Our human minds cannot fathom what all this embraces. Grace is whatever men and women need in order to be saved. It is exactly what men and women do not have, nor ever will have, of themselves.

In the God-man relationship, grace has two sides: grace that forgives and grace that empowers.[2] In Hebrew 4:16, for instance, Paul focused on the empowerment of grace: "Let us therefore come boldly to the throne of grace, that we may obtain mercy and find grace to help in time of need."

One of the indications of a limited gospel is an overemphasis on the mercies of grace with a muted glance at the empowerment of grace (whereby men and women find all the help they need to resist Satan). A limited understanding of grace leads to a false gospel and a misunderstanding of faith. A misunderstanding of faith leads to presumptuous assurance.

God will do all that an infinitely loving and patient lover can do to get His bride ready for the wedding of the universe (see Revelation 19:7-9). But there is something that even God cannot do—He can't force men and women to love Him! Love can never be forced!

All that a gracious God can do in wooing men and women is to appeal for their attention long enough to hear Him speak to their inmost thoughts, to listen to reason (see Isaiah 1:18). And the favorable response He seeks is called in the New Testament, "faith."

Faith is the human response to grace. Faith is that appreciation, appropriation, and acceptance of grace that opens the door for grace to continue its work in the life of the sinner. In short, faith permits grace to do its work.

Paul's classic definition (Ephesians 2:4) of the anatomy of salvation should have served as a barrier against two monstrous perversions that have divided Christian churches for centuries. On one hand, we have a large body of Christians who believe that grace covers men and women of faith in such a way that they are no longer "under the law" (Romans 6:15). On the other, we have Christians who believe worthy acts (so-called "acts of faith") in some way earn and/or satisfy God's love, and thus in some way help to secure their salvation.

The first group are called "antinomians," that is, they believe that grace "stands instead of the law." The second are often labeled as "legalists," those in bondage to "righteousness by works."

When grace is misunderstood, we immediately misunderstand faith. When we misunderstand faith, God's sovereignty and fairness—and thus His grace—is misunderstood.

Faith is the New Testament word that describes a person's free response to God's free grace. God made us, not as trees or animals, but as responsible persons, i.e., "able-to- respond." Thus, the meaning of "faith" depends on the kind of God we are relating to and how we understand human accountability.

If one thinks of God's sovereignty as meaning that no man or devil can thwart His will—that whatever God wants, He gets or does—then human beings can be no more than passive people, hardly more responsible than a dog. In such thinking, faith tends to become only a passive acceptance of what God has done. Human accountability is limited to an intellectual acceptance of His marvelous gift of grace. This "knowledge" is expressed in the joy of knowing that Jesus paid the price for one's salvation—and that nothing more can be, or needs to be, done to "add" to Christ's death on the cross. Logically and ethically (as history so sadly reveals) such thinking leads to a lessened regard for disciplined, obedient concern for growth in character. A cognitive disconnect exists between the sinner's need for help to overcome sin and the empowering role of the Holy Spirit in humankind's salvation.

But faith can be misunderstood from another direction. An overemphasis on the human side of the divine-human equation in Paul's anatomy of salvation, leads to an overemphasis on the reliability of reason and our emotional experiences. This overemphasis, though called faith, fails to grasp the magnitude and depth of sin. Such optimism believes, in some way, that a divine spark of goodness lodges within everyone, merely waiting for the touch of God to fan it. Many have gone down this road, assuming that humanity needs a teacher more than a Savior.

Here again a right definition of grace and faith will save us from these two errors—from an overemphasis on Jesus as our Savior that mutes His role as our Teacher-Example, on one hand, or on the other hand, from an overemphasis of His role as our Teacher and Example while muting His role as our Savior.

Dietrich Bonhoeffer, that heroic German pastor who showed all Christians how they should have responded to Nazi terror, spoke out plainly against these two perennial theological errors:

> The truth is that so long as we hold both sides of the proposition together they contain nothing inconsistent with right belief, but as soon as one is divorced from the other, it is bound to prove a stumbling-block. "Only those who believe [have faith] obey" . . . and "only those who obey believe [have faith]". . . . If the first half of the proposition stands alone, the believer is exposed to the danger of cheap grace, which is another word for damnation. If the second half stands alone, the believer is exposed to the danger of salvation through works, which is also another word for damnation.[3]

Bonhoeffer reminds me of a similar statement made by Ellen White as she commented on those who "expect to be saved by Christ's death, while they refuse to live His self-sacrificing life. They extol the riches of free grace, and attempt to cover themselves with an appearance of righteousness, hoping to screen their defects of character; but their efforts will be of no avail in the day of God."[4]

When faith is confused with mere belief, we have Christians who emphasize doctrine and orthodoxy of belief as the test of faith. Often their main refrain is "only believe."[5] Grace is then understood as God's all-encompassing gift of salvation "finished" on the cross without any human responsibility involved in character transformation.

When we confuse faith with cool reason or warm feelings, we have another large group that emphasizes good fellowship, warm harmony, and tolerance of belief because "all roads lead to heaven."[6] Grace then becomes a matter of believing in a very generous God who has many different mansions for the various religious groups of the world, all traveling up the mountain, but along different paths.[7]

It seems to me that this confusion of faith with the recognition of "common values" will be the driving force behind the prevailing threat and countervailing resistance in the end time to a church emphasizing the "commandments of God" and the "faith of Jesus" (Revelation 14:12). Whenever we emphasize "common values" the concern for doctrinal purity seems to fade. People will vote with their feet for a church that provides an exciting "experience," with hugging, lively praise songs devoid of content but captivating with beat and repetition, and a friendly "coffee hour."

We surely are not against a friendly church and relevant music. But when faith is divorced from the God that Jesus represented, all this activity becomes a substitute for a genuine, saving relationship with Jesus. The importance of biblical doctrine is considered divisive, thus unacceptable for a "loving" fellowship. In fact, to raise doctrinal issues, some say, would violate the rights of others to believe what they want. Whenever feelings replace facts, we have a rapidly swirling sinkhole that will increase in speed as the end of the end time draws nearer.

But now, back to the relationship between grace and faith—a clarity that is needed more and more wherever we look.

Mary Magdalene's experience is a cameo picture of how grace and faith work. We are told that she was converted and fell away—seven times (see Luke 8:2)! I suspect that most of us can relate in some way to Mary's struggles. It may not be lust and forbidden sexual pleasures, but everyone of us has some weakness that guardian angels would consider significant, even though we may not! And we can identify with Mary's determination to overcome these weaknesses!

Remember when Jesus stepped into Mary's life, saving her from being stoned to death (see John 8:3-12)? It was a frightful scene, with the
hypocrites getting their kicks out of putting Mary down for sins they
themselves participated in!

But Jesus had been working with weak Mary for some time. He
knew her heart; He "saw the better traits of her character." She "had
heard His strong cries to the Father in her behalf."[8] She knew she had
failed Him again and again and that she did not deserve another
chance.

But Jesus saw the picture differently. You know the story well. After writing incriminating information in the sand, He asked Mary
where her accusers were. Then Jesus showered grace on Mary, " 'Neither do I condemn you; go and sin no more' " (John 8:11). Grace met
both human need *and* Mary's responsibility. Grace does not, and would
not, keep Mary from sinning again without Mary's cooperation. Mary's
part was to respond to grace with faith.

Remember the occasion, later, in Simon's house, at a gathering of
the spiritually elite. Mary slipped in and indeed put Jesus in an awkward position—washing His feet with her tears and hair! Even kissing
His feet! It was an awkward situation for everyone present!

But for Mary, only Jesus mattered. She knew how weak and sordid
she had been— so did Jesus. But she also knew that the only Person in
the world who seemed to really care about her was this Teacher from
Nazareth. He was the only One who had treated her as if she might be
worth something. And she was grateful!

Jesus must have astonished the assembled guests by saying to Mary:
" 'Your sins are forgiven' " (Luke 7:48). But He was not finished: " 'Your
faith has saved you. Go in peace' " (verse 50). Can we find a better
example of grace and faith at work?

After that earlier temple experience when she had faced death,
Mary clung to Jesus' confidence in her. Day after day, she responded
to His confidence with everything that we have been saying about
faith. And now, in Simon's home, Jesus was recognizing her growth—
her victory over lust—and He commended her faith. "Mary, your faith
has saved you!"

That interchange with Mary may be the template for my life and
yours. How many times has Jesus said to you, "Your faith has saved
you!"? Not that you overcame all by yourself! Hardly! But Jesus could
not have "saved" you if you had not responded in faith, like Mary, to
His confidence in you. Faith is very, very important in our salvation.
Without faith, grace is not only frustrated, it is shut down as far as
you and I are concerned so that we cannot be saved.

Is there anything about your experience that is worse than Mary's? I doubt it. You, too, will find the sweetness of victory if you keep coming back to grace with your maturing faith, just as Mary did!

In other words, the God of grace initiates; men and women of faith respond. A gracious God explains; men and women of faith cooperate. The Lord of grace offers pardon and power,[9] and He waits for men and women of faith to freely grasp both. On His side, it is all grace, while on our side, it is all faith—faith that permits God's full authority to have His will done. Paul's anatomy of salvation could not have been said more clearly (see Ephesians 2:8).

From the first whisper of grace wooing sinners to seek their Savior, through the period of growth, until transformed sinners "reflect the image of Jesus fully,"[10] it is the same grace operating. It is God at work pursuing His original objective of changing sinners into "a new creation . . . so that in Him we might become the righteousness of God in Him" (2 Corinthians 5:17, 21).[11] The purpose of the gospel is reached— the restoration of the lost image of God in men and women of faith.

If we understood that the same grace and the same faith is functioning from the beginning of the Christian's commitment right through to his or her eventual "fitness"[12] for heaven, every theological problem dividing Christian groups today would vanish.

When faith claims God's gracious pardon in the noonday light of repentance (pardon/justification by faith), when faith claims God's gracious power in resisting evil from whatever source (power/sanctification by faith), it is the same quality of grace and faith operating. Bible writers make no distinction in grace or in faith between their functions in justification and sanctification. Ellen White, frequently, described this twin function of grace and faith without using conventional theological terms: "Freely will He pardon all who come to Him for forgiveness and restoration."[13] For Ellen White, the purpose of the gospel is always "restoration"[14]—the wonderful product of grace and faith.

What may seem to be a difference (faith receiving grace in either pardon or power) arises because one may be looking at faith as one would a windowpane. A person may see one side of the pane from the inside of the room; later, that same person my go outside and see the same window but through the other side of the pane. But it's the same windowpane! Men and women of faith, from one point of view, see faith as a passive response to God's grace—faith with its empty hands pleading for God's grace, for His mercies and pardon. But they also see faith as an active response—faith with its weak hands pleading for God's grace, for His power to overcome all hereditary and cultivated tendencies to sin.

We are not describing two kinds of faith any more than we are describing two separate pieces of glass, as if we could separate the windowpane into two separate pieces. Men and women of faith need and accept pardon and power because such gifts are exactly what men and women of faith know they need.

John Wesley, having seen all this clearly, became a bright beacon in his day amidst Calvinism in the Reformed denominations, on his right hand, and Arminianism, on his left. Note how he sorted all this out:

> By justification we are saved from the guilt of sin, and restored to the favor of God; by sanctification we are saved from the power and root of sin, and restored to the image of God. All experience, as well as Scripture, show this salvation to be both instantaneous and gradual. It begins the moment we are justified, in the holy, humble, gentle, patient love of God and man.[15]

The Reformed denominations (Calvinistic) taught that the elect only were given saving faith, that they would be justified by irresistible grace, and would be saved unconditionally. Most Arminians, in their emphasis on free grace and the free response of faith, erred in teaching that faith was unconditional. That is, they taught, in Wesley's words, that "Christ abolished the moral law . . . that Christian liberty is liberty from obeying the commandments of God, that it is a bondage to do a thing because it is commanded . . . that a Preacher ought not to exhort to good works; not unbelievers, because it is hurtful; not believers, because it is needless."[16] These two theological errors still divide every Christian denomination in the twenty-first century! All because of confusion regarding that one word, "faith." Out of that confusion we continue to have misunderstandings of grace, justification, sanctification, works, law, righteousness by faith, etc.

Wesley had to contend with those who thought he did not value justification highly enough because of his emphasis on sanctification. He had to resist those who thought he did not understand justification because he insisted on the growth of the moral life, the wholehearted obedience to the will of God.

For many years, Wesley emphasized, with Paul, that "faith is imputed for righteousness to every believer; namely, faith in the righteousness of Christ."

But Wesley always hastened to clarify what he and Paul meant when someone would ask, "Must not we put off the filthy rags of our own righteousness, before we can put on the spotless righteousness of Christ?" Wesley replied:

Certainly we must; that is, in plain terms, we must repent, before we can believe the gospel. We must be cut off from dependence upon ourselves, before we can truly depend on Christ. . . . But do not you believe inherent righteousness? Yes, in its proper place; not as the ground of our acceptance with God, but as the fruit of it; not in the place of imputed righteousness, but as consequent upon it. That is, I believe God implants righteousness in every one to whom he has imputed it. . . .

In the meantime, what we are afraid of is this—lest any should use the phrase, "The righteousness of Christ," or, "The righteousness of Christ is imputed to me," as a cover for his unrighteousness. We have known this done a thousand times. A man has been reproved, suppose for drunkenness: "O," said he, "I pretend to no righteousness *of my own;* Christ is *my righteousness.*" Another has been told, that "the extortioner, the unjust, shall not inherit the kingdom of God;" He replies, with all assurance, "I am unjust in myself, but I have a spotless righteousness in Christ." And thus, though a man be as far from the practice as from the tempers of a Christian; though he neither has the mind which was in Christ, nor in any respect walks as He walked; yet, he has armour of proof against all conviction, in what he calls "the righteousness of Christ."

It is the seeing of so many deplorable instances of this kind, which makes us sparing in the use of these expressions.[17]

In reviewing all this, we must be crystal clear: even though faith is prompted by God, faith is not God's work but ours—the human response to God's call for men and women to represent Him in proving Satan wrong. For men and women to respond to God's wooing, God must wait. He cannot, by the nature of His character, force faith. He can appeal to faith; He can win it, but never coerce it. He does not even give "grace to help in time of need" (Hebrews 4:16) if it is not asked for! Even as He does not give the grace of forgiveness unless it is asked for by the sincerely repentant, those who confess and forsake their sins (see Proverbs 28:13; 1 John 1:9)![18]

In other words, faith is an attitude of saying "Yes" to grace—to whatever God wants us to say or do. For that reason we speak of the experience of faith as God's way of reestablishing the reign of love (see Galatians 5:6). Faith is not genuine, is not complete, unless it produces a truly loving person, and that remarkable development is a result of grace at work.[19]

John Wesley could easily be called the Preacher of Love.[20] Of all the major Protestant Reformers, Wesley understood most clearly the plan of salvation. He saw the correct connection between grace, faith, and love:

> Faith, then, was originally designed of God to re-establish the law of love. Therefore, in speaking thus, we are not undervaluing it, or robbing it of its due praise; but, on the contrary, showing its real worth, exalting it in its just proportion, and giving it that very place which the wisdom of God assigned it from the beginning. It is the grand means of restoring that holy love wherein man was originally created. It follows, that although faith is of no value in itself, (as neither is any other means whatsoever,) yet as it leads to that end, the establishing anew the law of love in our hearts; and as, in the present state of things, it is the only means under heaven for effecting it; it is on that account an unspeakable blessing to man, and of unspeakable value before God.[21]

Both Wesley and Ellen White, at the core of their theologies, are motivated by Paul's message to the Galatians: "For we through the Spirit eagerly wait for the hope of righteousness by faith. For in Christ Jesus neither circumcision nor uncircumcision avails anything, but faith working through love" (Galatians 5:5, 6).

Thus, through men and women of faith the universe sees the intrinsic reality of the plan of salvation manifested, validated, and vindicated. When God goes about providing grace to men and women of faith, it is an ethical matter and not merely a judicial act leading to legal fiction. The gospel is concerned about redemption, not legal transactions. Grace liberates men and women of faith from their sins by helping them to overcome them, not cover them by some kind of theological magic or legal fiction—and then call all this, "righteousness by faith."[22]

Paul urges us all "not to receive the grace of God in vain. . . . Since we have these promises, beloved, let us cleanse ourselves from all filthiness of the flesh and spirit, perfecting holiness in the fear of God" (2 Corinthians 6:1; 7:1).

Mildred Wynkoop said it well: "Men [and women] are always trying to find some way to escape personal responsibility for being what they are, and to avoid having to confess it and do something about it. . . . They (or we) are seeking an escape from inner evil in some magical way that evades the mature demand of meeting moral demands head on."[23]

I know that some readers are wondering about all this, fearing that we may be unconsciously introducing human "works" into the salvation equation. Let's talk about that in our next chapter.

---

[1] See chapter 8.

[2] Again, note the clear use of the ellipse of salvation—pardon and power.

[3] *The Cost of Discipleship* (New York: The Macmillan Company, 1959, hardback), p. 58.

[4] *Christ's Object Lessons*, p. 316.

[5] See pp. 59, 60

[6] "Do you want a special feeling or emotion to prove that Christ is yours? Is this more reliable than pure faith in God's promises? Would it not be better to take the blessed promises of God and apply them to yourself, bearing your whole weight upon them? This is faith" (Ellen G. White, *Review and Herald*, July 29, 1890).

"We can see the importance, then, of having true faith, for it is the motive power of the Christian's life and action; but feeling is not faith; emotion is not faith. We must bring our very work and thought and emotions to the test of the word, and true faith will be profoundly impressed by the voice of God, and will act accordingly. If people would only search the Scriptures more diligently, false doctrines and heresies would be fewer" (Ellen G. White, *Signs of the Times,* November 24, 1887).

"Genuine faith is founded on the Scriptures; but Satan uses so many devices to wrest the Scriptures and bring in error, that great care is needed if one would know what they really do teach. It is one of the great delusions of this time to dwell much upon feeling, and to claim honesty while ignoring the plain utterances of the word of God because that word does not coincide with feeling. Many have no foundation for their faith but emotion. Their religion consists in excitement; when that ceases, their faith is gone. Feeling may be chaff, but the word of God is the wheat. And 'what,' says the prophet, 'is the chaff to the wheat'?" (Ellen G. White, *Review and Herald*, November 25, 1884).

[7] Here is a sample of what we can read in any newspaper or newsmagazine, several times a week: "The key to finding the balance of truth found in all spiritual paths and that accommodates varying religious beliefs is the recognition that each religion contains elements of truth. By accepting this principle, we are then free to view each religion as a spiritual path to the infinite, eternal, and omnipotent divine source of all things. We can each follow our own path; share our faith with others without hatred, scorn, or violence; and accept others' paths as equally valid to our own" (Letter to the Editor, *U.S. News & World Report,* June 24, 2002).

[8] Ellen G. White, *The Desire of Ages*, p. 568.

[9] See Ellen G. White, *Education*, p. 36.

[10] Ellen G. White, *Early Writings*, p. 71.

[11] "God was to be manifest in Christ, 'reconciling the world unto Himself.' 2 Corinthians 5:19. Man had become so degraded by sin that it was impossible for him, in himself, to come into harmony with Him whose nature is purity and goodness. But Christ, after having redeemed man from the condemnation of the law, could impart divine power to unite with human effort. Thus by repentance toward God and faith in Christ the fallen children of Adam might once more become 'sons of God' (1 John 3:2)" (Ellen G. White, *Patriarchs and Prophets*, p. 64).

[12] "Fitness," see Ellen G. White, *Christ's Object Lessons*, pp. 96, 221, 288, 307, 309, 310, 312, 355, 356, 360, 384, 408, 412.

[13] *The Desire of Ages,* p. 568.

[14] See *Education,* pp. 15, 16.

[15] Wesley, John, *The Works of John Wesley,* Third Edition (Kansas City, Mo: Beacon Hill Press, 1978), vol. VII, p. 509.

[16] Wesley, op. cit., vol. VIII, p. 278.

[17] Wesley, op. cit., vol. V, pp. 241, 244.

[18] We must not confuse "repentance" with "coming to Jesus." The precious word, *come,* especially when the sinner sees God's love through Jesus on the cross, is the pulling power that breaks the sinner's heart. In other words, the remorseful sinner "must go to Christ in order that he may be enabled to repent" (Ellen G. White, *Review and Herald,* September 3, 1901). "Just here is a point on which many may err, and hence they fail of receiving the help that Christ desires to give them. They think that they cannot come to Christ unless they first repent, and that repentance prepares for the forgiveness of their sins. It is true that repentance does precede the forgiveness of sins; for it is only the broken and contrite heart that will feel the need of a Savior. But must the sinner wait till he has repented before he can come to Jesus? Is repentance to be made an obstacle between the sinner and the Savior? The Bible does not teach that the sinner must repent before he can heed the invitation of Christ, 'Come unto Me, all ye that labor and are heavy laden, and I will give you rest' (Matthew 11:28). It is the virtue that goes forth from Christ that leads to genuine repentance" (Ellen G. White, *Steps to Christ,* p. 26).

[19] "Genuine faith always works by love. When you look to Calvary it is not to quiet your soul in the non-performance of duty, not to compose yourself to sleep, but to create faith in Jesus, faith that will work, purifying the soul from the slime of selfishness. When we lay hold of Christ by faith, our work has just begun. Every man has corrupt and sinful habits that must be overcome by vigorous warfare. Every soul is required to fight the fight of faith. If one is a follower of Christ, he cannot be sharp in deal, he cannot be hardhearted, devoid of sympathy. He cannot be coarse in his speech. He cannot be full of pomposity and self-esteem. He cannot be overbearing, nor can he use harsh words, and censure and condemn. The labor of love springs from the work of faith" (Ellen G. White, *Seventh-day Adventist Bible Commentary,* vol. 6, p. 1111).

[20] One of the most compelling reviews of John Wesley's theology has been written by Mildred Bangs Wynkoop, *A Theology of Love: The Dynamic of Wesleyanism* (Kansas City, Mo: Beacon Hill Press, 1972).

[21] Wesley, op. cit., vol. V, p. 464.

[22] "The religion of Christ means more than the forgiveness of sin; it means taking away our sins, and filling the vacuum with the graces of the Holy Spirit. It means divine illumination, rejoicing in God. It means a heart emptied of self, and blessed with the abiding presence of Christ. When Christ reigns in the soul, there is purity, freedom from sin. The glory, the fullness, the completeness of the gospel plan is fulfilled in the life. The acceptance of the Savior brings a glow of perfect peace, perfect love, perfect assurance. The beauty and fragrance of the character of Christ revealed in the life testifies that God has indeed sent His Son into the world to be its Savior" (Ellen G. White, *Christ's Object Lessons,* pp. 419, 420).

[23] Wynkoop, op. cit., p. 164.

CHAPTER TEN

But What About "Works"?

Obviously, we should have no discussion about assurance, faith, and grace without discussing "works"—that New Testament word that helped to focus the hostility between the Jews and early Christians. Disagreements over what Paul or James meant by "works," or "righteousness by works," has continued to divide Christians to this day. Is it a matter of definitions only or does it involve different ways of looking at the gospel?

Either way, it surely affects why many people have difficulty finding the "assurance of faith" (Hebrews 10:22).

Paul says, "A man is not justified by the works of the law but by faith in Jesus Christ" (Galatians 2:16). And he further declares, "We conclude that a man is justified by faith apart from the deeds of the law" (Romans 3:28).

But James said: "You see then that a man is justified by works, and not by faith only . . . for as the body without the spirit is dead, so faith without works is dead also" (2:24, 26).

What shall we make of this apparent contradiction? It has much to do with our understanding of the "assurance of salvation." If you don't believe me, ask anyone who is confused or unsettled about his or her assurance of salvation.

The first step in resolving this apparent contradiction is to remember the purpose of the gospel and how God plans to make the universe eternally secure. Because the purpose of the gospel is to "restore in man the image of his Maker" and because only loyal, obedient men and women of faith can guarantee an eternally secure universe, any discussion of the assurance of faith and "works" must focus on the end product—the transformed rebel who can be safe to save.[1]

Our second step is to understand what the context was for Paul and for James when they made their apparently contradictory statements. We know what they said, but what did they mean?

James was primarily concerned with the misunderstanding of faith. That same misunderstanding has troubled the Christian church from the first century to ours. John Wesley faced the same problem—unconditional faith that viewed the law of God to be no longer binding on those who were "under grace" (Romans 6:15).[2] James is exceedingly clear regarding the authority of God's law, especially the Ten Commandments (see James 2:8-12).[3]

James understood the gospel; he was a lucid teacher. He not only clarified the binding authority of the Ten Commandments, he drilled home the clearest statement regarding sin in the Bible: "Therefore, to him who knows to do good and does not do it, to him it is sin" (James 4:17). He gave no comfort to those who believed that genuine faith was no longer subject to the Ten Commandments or to any other expression of the will of God.

The book of James has been a profound source of strength for serious Christians through the years. He wrote during tough times. He saw his colleagues killed for the truth, and he knew he was on martyrdom's short list. But listen to him sing, "Count it all joy when you fall into various trials, knowing that the testing of your faith produces patience ["endurance" (Greek); compare Revelation 14:12], but let patience ["endurance"] have its perfect work, that you may be perfect and complete lacking nothing" (James 1:2-4). Those are words of one who had the assurance of salvation, day by day.

James's message is full of counsel about how to endure and to receive the "crown of life" (James 1:12): "Therefore lay aside all filthiness and overflow of wickedness, and receive with meekness the implanted word, which is able to save your souls. But be doers of the word, and not hearers only, deceiving yourselves" (James 1:21, 22).

I think James is echoing his Lord's searing warning that ended the Sermon on the Mount: " 'Not everyone who says to Me, "Lord, Lord," shall enter the kingdom of heaven, but he who does the will of My Father in heaven' " (Matthew 7:21).

The book of James is worth a reread every year at least. He warns against "cheap grace" and against the bewitching slogan, "Only believe!" For James, faith was the wholehearted response to God's grace—the heart appreciation that is grateful for forgiveness and eager for God's power to help in overcoming the sins that need to be forgiven.

Now back to Paul. How could Paul be against James's sturdy appeal? Of course, Paul is not contradicting James. Paul was talking about a different issue when he targeted "works" as the wrong way to find harmony with God and His righteousness. Paul was answering the same question that James addressed: How do we become righteous and holy, "without which no one will see the Lord" (Hebrews 12:14)? But he was looking at the question from another direction.

Paul emphatically agreed with James that it was an error for a person to consider himself righteous and holy by believing that Jesus did all that was necessary for his salvation on the cross, that Jesus' grace now covered his unholy life because Jesus had kept the law for him (see Romans 6–8; 1 Corinthians 15:34; 2 Corinthians 7:1).

The first error Paul aimed at

But Paul aimed at another fundamental problem that has plagued men and women since Cain killed Abel—especially those who believe that they are God's chosen people! The problem is this: Those who sincerely try to make themselves righteous and holy by strenuous religious effort.

Paul saw it in the Jewish rituals of his earlier religious experience; no matter how hard one tries, no matter how many holy places one visits, no matter how much "self-imposed religion, false humility, and neglect of the body" (Colossians 2:23), a person can never restore himself in the image of his Maker, never convince the angels or beings on other worlds or God that he should be trusted with eternal life based on his actions.

Religious people obviously do religious things, such as following strict dietary habits, being careful in Sabbath observance (especially what we *don't* do), tithing scrupulously, withdrawing from worldly pleasures, etc. In other words, many sincere religious people can say with Paul, as he looked back on his former, exemplary life as a Jewish leader, "concerning the righteousness which is in the law, [I was] blameless" (Philippians 3:6)!

Because Paul knew all this firsthand, He took dead aim on this kind of "righteousness which is in the law." This is what he calls "the works of the law" (Galatians 3:5) or his "own righteousness, which is from the law" (Philippians 3:9). It should be obvious that Paul's context is light years away from what James was concerned with.

In Galatians especially, Paul is dealing with the confusion that some Jewish Christians were dumping on new believers. In a way, they had some logic and appeal—or they wouldn't have had anybody listening to them! The main issue was circumcision, a God-given command to the father of the faithful, Abraham himself. And who wouldn't want to be a "child" of Abraham! For the Jewish male, circumcision was the gold standard for the "assurance of faith"! A perfect example of why "works" today, whatever that external duty may be, carries with it a sense of assurance—but it is presumptuous assurance!

The problem was that the significance of this rite had been lost through the centuries. Instead of a sign of heart commitment, it had become a loyalty test much as some today view saluting the flag. No salute—unpatriotic; no circumcision—an unbeliever!

Paul's argument was that after Jesus came, believers no longer needed circumcision to identify them as believers. Christian baptism had replaced circumcision as the outward sign of loyalty to God: "In Him you were also circumcised with the circumcision made without hands, by putting off the body of the sins of the flesh, by the circumcision of Christ, buried with Him in baptism, in which you also were raised with Him through faith in the working of God, who raised Him from the dead" (Colossians 2:11, 12; see also Ephesians 2:11-15).

But baptism can become as devoid of meaning for Christians as circumcision had become to the Jews. For many Christians, baptism has become one of their "evidences" that they are, already, among the *ultimately saved!*

Paul's use of the phrase "works of the law" referred to those in the church who were insisting (1) that Christians should also "observe days and months and seasons and years [Old Testament sanctuary observances]" (Galatians 4:10) and (2) that Gentiles should be circumcised: "Indeed I, Paul, say to you that if you become circumcised, Christ will profit you nothing. And I testify again to every man who becomes circumcised that he is a debtor to keep the whole law [the Mosaic law]. You have become estranged from Christ, you who attempt to be justified by law; you have fallen from grace. . . . For in Christ Jesus neither circumcision nor uncircumcision avails anything but faith working through love" (Galatians 5:2-6).

This question of circumcision kept the early church in turmoil (see, for example, Acts 15). Paul called it "a yoke of bondage" (Galatians 5:1; see Acts 15:10).

Why were Paul and other Christian leaders so adamant regarding "the works of the law," calling them "a yoke of bondage" which "neither our fathers nor we were able to bear" (Acts 15:10)?

This leads us into the deeper meaning behind "works of the law." Paul was not limiting this phrase to circumcision only, though that issue became the lightning rod of contention. What really stunned the Galatians (and Christians ever since who want to grasp Paul's dramatic Matterhorn view of faith) was that he was including *all law,* even the Ten Commandments, in his phrase, "works of the law."[4] This must have been the theological hydrogen bomb that echoed throughout the early Christian church; it still has a blockbuster impact in many Christian churches today. No wonder the "Jewish Party" was scandalized!

Without a correct understanding of the meaning of Paul's entire argument in his letter to the Galatians, Christians even today remain confused. They are reluctant to include the Ten Commandments within "works of the law" (as Paul used the phrase in the Galatian letter).

The second error Paul aimed at

Why is this so? This leads us into the second error Paul was concerned about when he wrote against "the works of the law." He could see that both Jews and some early Christians were *misunderstanding the difference between the old and new covenants.* More later.

However, Paul does not finish his Galatian letter without explaining just what he meant by this startling concept that keeping the Ten Commandments should be included in his condemnation of the "works of the law." He certainly was not an antinomian (one who believes that grace and faith substitutes for our obedience)!

Clearly, Paul was not downgrading the authority of the Ten Commandments. Hardly! Not Paul who would write: "The law is holy, and the commandment holy and just and good" (Romans 7:12). Or, "Awake to righteousness, and do not sin; for some do not have the knowledge of God" (1 Corinthians 15:34). Or, "For we must all appear before the judgment seat of Christ; that each one may receive the things done in the body, according to what he has done, whether good or bad" (2 Corinthians 5:10).

Paul, in Romans and Galatians, was clarifying the role of *law,* even the Ten Commandments which he said "gives birth to bondage" (Galatians 4:24). To the Romans he wrote that one of the purposes of the law is to provide "the knowledge of sin" (Romans 3:20).

As a result, *law,* even the Ten Commandment law, can provide the honest worshiper with only "wretchedness" and the sense of living with "the body of death" (Romans 7:24). Paul knew by experience that "keeping the law [external obedience]" provided the security of "righteousness which is from the law" (Philippians 3:9). But when he heard the gospel and called Jesus his Lord, all the good works of the law he "counted loss for Christ" and "as rubbish" (Philippians 3:7, 8).

That new experience of finding grace—grace in freely-given pardon and power—lifted Paul from the burden of works-righteousness to the joy of "the righteousness which is from God by faith" (Philippians 3:9). No longer did sin have to reign. Paul could sing to the Romans: "For you are not under law [the yoke that reveals sin] but under grace [the grace of pardon and power]" (Romans 6:14).[5]

Then Paul uses an interesting metaphor: Before the gospel, they were sinners and could do nothing about it; they were *slaves* to their desires. After the gospel, they were "obey[ing] from the heart that form of doctrine to which you were delivered. And having been set free from sin, you became . . . *slaves* of righteousness for holiness. . . . But now having been set free from sin, and having become *slaves* of God, you have your fruit to holiness, and the end, everlasting life" (Romans 6:17-22).[6]

Now let's pick up our earlier reference to the old and new covenants. The old covenant does not describe a time period (such as from Sinai to the Cross) but an attitude that reflects reliance on external obedience to law without the heart's transformation that produces "the fruits of the Spirit."[7]

Thus, the experiences of the *new* and the *old* covenants are like parallel tracks running from Abel and Cain to the Second Advent.[8] The two covenants are "heart-experience related," not "time related." The difference between an honest person wearing the "yoke of bondage" of the old covenant and an honest person within the joy of the new covenant is the experience of faith. Paul was honest while burdened with the bondage of external commandment keeping—the old covenant experience. Paul was also honest, but relieved and at peace when he came to realize the joy of knowing that God freely forgives and empowers his honest commitment to doing God's will—the new covenant experience.

What makes the difference between the two covenants? Genuine faith makes the difference. Only a correct understanding of faith can bring real peace and real victory in a Christian's life (see Romans 5:1, 2). Only a correct understanding of faith in relation to the works of the law can guarantee one's assurance of faith.

All this may sound too abstract, too theological. How does this all work so that the average, nontheological man or woman can easily understand how to get right and stay right with His Lord, so that they can "work . . . His good pleasure"?[9] And how does all this clarify one's assurance of faith?

Peter spoke to the average person: "So then, have your minds ready for action. Keep alert and set your hope completely on the blessing which will be given you when Jesus Christ is revealed. Be obedient to God, and do not allow your lives to be shaped by those desires you had when you were still ignorant. Instead, be holy in all that you do, just as God who called you is holy. The scripture says, 'Be holy because I am holy' " (1 Peter 1:13, 14, TEV).

To the Thessalonians, Paul wrote: "Finally, our brothers, you learnt from us how you should live in order to please God. This is, of course, how you have been living. And now we beg and urge you in the name of the Lord Jesus to do even more" (1 Thessalonians 4:1, 2, TEV).

To the Philippians, Paul emphasized his interest in pleasing God: "Therefore [in view of Christ's example and ministry] . . . work out your own salvation with fear and trembling; for it is God who works in you both to will and to do for His good pleasure. Do all things without murmuring and disputing, that you may become blameless and harmless, children of God without fault in the midst of a crooked and perverse generation, among whom you shine as lights in the world" (Philippians 2:12-15).

God's "good pleasure" is our salvation! Restoring His universe in such a way that no angel or human being would ever again want to think a rebellious thought—that would be God's good pleasure! Enjoying the eternal security of all His creation—that would be God's good pleasure!

But, are Peter and Paul's admonitions being made clear these days? It doesn't seem so! Many voices in all churches insist that to focus on the Christian life (that is, on sanctification), is to emphasize behaviorism, even legalism! That to include sanctification within "righteousness by faith" is to retreat to Rome and papal doctrine![10] Some say that to ask for holy lives as part of the gospel message is to lay a crushing burden on "saved" Christians. This burden, they say, leads to frustration, perhaps even to despair. After all, the argument runs, "Who is holy?" Or "Show me a perfect person!"

So, I ask the question: Are the apostles (and God) asking the impossible when they call us to "work out" our salvation—to "be holy"? Is this so-called impossible goal really God's will? Perhaps the marketers of the Lexus automobile may understand all this better than some Christians when they emblazon their motto the world over: "The relentless pursuit of perfection!"

Isn't it interesting? To suggest that God is asking the impossible is to repeat exactly what Satan has been saying from the beginning—and what he has artfully confused the minds of many professed Christians to believe! Truly, Satan is the grand deceiver and master liar (see Revelation 12:7; John 8:44)!

Observe Ellen White's counsel:

Through defects in the character, Satan works to gain control of the whole mind, and he knows that if these defects are cherished, he will succeed. Therefore he is constantly seeking to deceive the followers of Christ with his fatal sophistry that it is impossible for them to overcome.[11]

Further:

Satan has asserted that men could not keep the commandments of God. To prove that they could, Christ became a man, and lived a life of perfect obedience, an evidence to sinful human beings, to the worlds unfallen, and to the heavenly angels, that man could keep God's law through the divine power that is abundantly provided for all that believe. In order to reveal God to the world, to demonstrate as true that which Satan has denied, Christ volunteered to take humanity, and in His power, humanity can obey God.[12]

Many Christians have found psychological relief in Satan's lies; too often we believe what our desires want us to believe. Their theological excuses go in several directions:

- The cross of Christ canceled the demands of the law, placing all believers under grace.
- Trying to keep the law is unnecessary because Jesus kept the law for us and He is our Substitute.
- Trying to keep the law is a foolish attempt because overcoming sin completely is not possible while we still live in sinful flesh.
- Trying to keep the law leads either to frustration, despair, or legalism.
- This emphasis on Jesus being our Example goes too far because, they say, He was exempt from His mother's DNA and genetic code—thus, asking humans to "perfectly reflect His character" is asking for the impossible.

However, these theological excuses arising from psychological desires are attempts to evade the clear call of Jesus: " 'Therefore whoever hears these sayings of Mine, and does them, I will liken him to a wise man who built his house on the rock' " (Matthew 7:24).

Jesus came to earth, not only to be our loving Savior, but also to give humanity His example. Even more, He gave us a clear picture of the Holy Spirit's job description[13]—to give us the power and courage to beat Satan down, just as He did in human flesh.[14] Bible writers were unified and clear that Christians have the same resources available that Jesus had so that all Christians may overcome, " 'as I [Jesus] also overcame' " (Revelation 3:21). Jesus came to demolish our excuses!

Let the Bible speak to us. Let's hear what Paul heard and passed on to fellow Christians—for example, Hebrews 2:17, 4:15. Let's remove the filters of theological debate and commentaries. Let simple words speak directly, personally, quietly, to our souls. Let's review unambiguous counsel in the writings of Ellen White on why Jesus came and why He died.

Ponder what Jesus meant when He said, " 'Strive to enter through the narrow gate' " (Luke 13:24). Selfish, rebellious people cannot inherit the kingdom of God because they carry too many excuses with them—they look for a wider gate! However, the good news, the clearest, most consistent bottom line of Scripture, hammered home from Genesis to Revelation, is that God has supplied whatever we need to get through the "narrow gate."

But we must be clear as to how all this works! We all know how persistently weak we are. Is it a matter of developing our willpower—of simply striving harder? No! Never! God has given us a better plan—a plan that works whenever we buy into it!

That is why the Holy Spirit led Peter to write:

> His divine power has given to us all things that pertain to life and godliness, through the knowledge of Him who called us by glory and virtue, by which have been given to us exceedingly great and precious promises, that through these you may be partakers of the divine nature, having escaped the corruption that is in the world through lust (2 Peter 1:3, 4).

Note that God does not push us out of the driver's seat. He does not do the driving for us. God's terrific goal for us is that we should be responsible, predictable, trustworthy drivers of our lives—persons made safe to drive the highways of the hereafter, made worthy by His infinite grace.[15] And His terrific promise is that He will supply whatever we need to be "good drivers."[16] That's plenty of reason to live joyfully in the assurance of salvation!

Now, back to Philippians 2:12, 13. Here Paul is telling us how God will make us safe drivers, here and forever—how we "may be partakers of the divine nature, having escaped the corruption that is in the world through lust." In other words, how our "works" (with the right motivation) should cooperate with the Holy Spirit in making us overcomers (good and safe drivers)!

Here Paul gives us the formula for overcoming our self-centered habit patterns, inherited or acquired: *Our will + God's grace = overcomers who fulfill God's "good pleasure"!* In this life? Absolutely. It's the only one we have. There is no second chance after death—we are having our second chances every day we wake up. In this life we seal our destiny. In fact, every day we are becoming either more mature wheat or more mature tares (see Matthew 13:24-30).

It's the relentless appeal of the book of Revelation: " 'To him who overcomes I will give to eat from the tree of life' " (2:7); " 'He who overcomes shall not be hurt by the second death' " (2:11); " 'To him who overcomes I will give some of the hidden manna to eat' " (2:17); " 'He who overcomes, and keeps My works until the end, to him I will give power over the nations' " (2:26); " 'He who overcomes shall be clothed in white garments' " (3:5); " 'He who overcomes, I will make him a pillar in the temple of My God' " (3:12); " 'To him who overcomes I will grant to sit with Me on My throne' " (3:21). All that takes my breath away!

To make this business of overcoming even more relevant, realistic, and desirable to each of us today, especially to those who live in the end of the end time, let's listen carefully to this blazing statement:

> When He comes He is not to cleanse us of our sins, to remove from us the defects in our characters, or to cure us of the infirmities of our tempers and dispositions. If wrought for us at all, this work will all be accomplished before that time. When the Lord comes, those who are holy will be holy still. Those who have preserved their bodies and spirits in holiness, in sanctification and honor, will then receive the finishing touch of immortality. But those who are unjust, unsanctified, and filthy will remain so forever. No work will then be done for them to remove their defects and give them holy characters. The Refiner does not then sit to pursue His refining process and remove their sins and their corruption. This is all to be done in these hours of probation. It is now that this work is to be accomplished for us. . . .
>
> As we come under the influence of that truth, it will accomplish the work for us which is necessary to give us a moral fitness for the kingdom of glory and for the society of the heavenly angels. We are now in God's workshop. Many of us are rough stones from the quarry. But as we lay hold upon the truth of God, its influence affects us. It elevates us and removes from us every imperfection and sin, of whatever nature.

Thus we are prepared to see the King in His beauty and finally to unite with the pure and heavenly angels in the kingdom of glory. It is here that this work is to be accomplished for us, here that our bodies and spirits are to be fitted for immortality.[17]

We have just read a very sobering description of reality. When our probation closes, there are no replays! No mulligans! No second editions! That statement deserves a rereading. It reflects Paul's formula: *Our will + God's grace = overcomers, who fulfill God's "good pleasure."*

Our part of the formula is spelled out in many ways in the New Testament: " 'strive' " (Luke 13:24); "put off the old man" (Colossians 3:9); "be diligent" (Hebrews 4:11); "lay aside every weight and the sin which so easily ensnares us, and let us run with endurance" (Hebrews 12:1); "resist the devil" (James 4:7). These are only samples!

Now for God's part: He will provide "grace to help in time of need" (Hebrews 4:16) so that we should "be strengthened with might through His Spirit in the inner man . . . according to the power that works in us" (Ephesians 3:16, 20). He "is able to keep you from stumbling and to present you faultless before the presence of His glory" (Jude 24).

A noonday sun description of how Paul's formula works in our lives is found in that helpful book, *Messages to Young People:*

> While these youth [Hebrew young men] were working out their own salvation, God was working in them to will and to do of His good pleasure. Here are revealed the conditions of success. To make God's grace our own, we must act our part. The Lord does not propose to perform for us either the willing or the doing. His grace is given to work in us to will and to do, but never as a substitute for our effort. Our souls are to be aroused to co-operate. The Holy Spirit works in us, that we may work out our own salvation. This is the practical lesson the Holy Spirit is striving to teach us. "It is God which worketh in you both to will and to do of His good pleasure."[18]

To highlight the biblical view of God's divine-human co-op plan, my favorite author could not be clearer:

> The work of gaining salvation is one of co-partnership, a joint operation. There is to be co-operation between God and the repentant sinner. This is necessary for the formation of right principles in the character. Man is to make earnest efforts to overcome that which hinders him from attaining to perfection. But

he is wholly dependent upon God for success. Human effort of itself is not sufficient. Without the aid of divine power it avails nothing. God works and man works. Resistance of temptation must come from man, who must draw his power from God. . . .

God wishes us to have the mastery over ourselves. But He cannot help us without our consent and co-operation. The divine Spirit works through the powers and faculties given to man. Of ourselves, we are not able to bring the purposes and desires and inclinations into harmony with the will of God; but if we are "willing to be made willing," the Savior will accomplish this for us. . . . Day by day God works with him, perfecting the character that is to stand in the time of final test. And day by day the believer is working out before men and angels a sublime experiment, showing what the gospel can do for fallen human beings.[19]

How could we ever hope to have more help than that? He takes our weak willingness and begins His "sublime experiment." Not just a few favorites. You and I are His projects, and He is very good at what He does. Whatever your dark moments, your failed attempts to gratify self—Jesus begins again where you are. The same compassion (Greek: "gut feelings") He had for so many in Palestine as He walked among humans, He feels for you. Not only does He feel viscerally for you, He can do something about it that no human surgeon or psychiatrist could ever hope to do. He wants the universe to see what you and He can do together in working out this "sublime experiment, showing what the gospel can do for fallen human beings."

Looking again at Paul's classic formula for the overcomer, we find an interesting concept: "work . . . with fear and trembling" (Philippians 2:12). What could Paul possibly mean? For one thing, he is not throwing a dark cloud over the striving Christian. Nor is he placing the Christian in the impossible position of Sisyphus—always rolling the huge rock up the hill, only to have it roll back again just as he reaches the top, again and again!

When God cooperates with our best efforts, no one needs to fear failure. God always lives up to His promises. He will never grow weary of picking us up, any more than parents grow impatient with their child learning to walk. That is why those with the "assurance of faith" (Hebrews 10:22) have a built-in melody that keeps them singing even when dark clouds seem to smother them.

I know, Paul did mention "fear and trembling." Let's see how fear has its place in working out our salvation. Remember how Solomon put it: "In the fear of the Lord there is strong confidence. . . . The fear of the Lord is a fountain of life" (Proverbs 14:26, 27).[20]

Don't we all fear embarrassing our closest friends or anyone who trusts us? I know that I fear embarrassing my wife or my children. I fear misusing the trust that people have in me, trust that has been built up over the years. I fear that I could mislead somebody with hasty words in a sermon. Above all, I fear that I will say or do something that will not "hallow" our Lord's name.

Why? Because I fear punishment? Maybe, but that is not the greatest fear. The greatest fear is to look into faces that I have "let down." Perhaps the following counsel will help us:

> God does not bid you fear that He will fail to fulfill His promises, that His patience will weary, or His compassion be found wanting. Fear lest your will shall not be held in subjection to Christ's will, lest your hereditary and cultivated traits of character shall control your life. "It is God which worketh in you both to will and to do of His good pleasure." Fear lest self shall interpose between your soul and the great Master Worker. Fear lest self-will shall mar the high purpose that through you God desires to accomplish. Fear to trust to your own strength, fear to withdraw your hand from the hand of Christ and attempt to walk life's pathway without His abiding presence.[21]

This life of cooperation with the mind and power of God, this working out of God's "good pleasure," this life of abiding in Christ, is what Paul calls "the righteousness from God that depends on faith" (Philippians 3:9, RSV). This quiet, but sure, basis for assurance of faith provides the foundation for the daily sense of a saving fellowship with Jesus.

But we still have that lingering question: How does God's power work His will within us? The work of the Holy Spirit, the indwelling Energizer, is the key, the open secret, to Paul's salvation formula regarding our part and God's part in working out our salvation.

Strange to say, but the primary function of the Holy Spirit has been rarely described throughout the Christian era! Along with His work as the Convincer of sin, as the helpful Tutor as we read the Bible, His highest purpose, toward which all other functions focus, is to reproduce in us the character of Jesus. This is the only way the Holy Spirit (or anyone else) can truly witness to Jesus: " 'The Spirit of truth, who proceeds from the Father, He will testify of Me' " (John 15:26). We witness to Jesus by letting the Holy Spirit do His work in us![22]

Perhaps this has never been stated more clearly than in the following:

> The Holy Spirit is the breath of spiritual life in the soul.
> The impartation of the Spirit is the impartation of the life of
> Christ. It imbues the receiver with the attributes of Christ.
> Only those who are thus taught of God, those who possess the
> inward working of the Spirit, and in whose life the Christ-life
> is manifested, are to stand as representative men, to minister
> in behalf of the church.[23]

Never will the time come when we will no longer need the friendly energy of the Holy Spirit. Until the Christian dies, or until after the close of probation in the last days, every genuine, faithful Christian will feel the appeal of sin, the tug of Satan, even as Jesus did—even to the end of His earthly life in Gethsemane and on Calvary.

Now let's get practical—where does the Holy Spirit "get into" our lives? At what point does He intersect with me and you? Surely not through our fingernails or liver!

This fact is one of the most essential truths we could ever know: Our "brain nerves . . . are the medium through which heaven communicates with man." And this connection "affects the inmost life." Now the obvious: "Whatever hinders the circulation of the electric current in the nervous system, thus weakening the vital powers and lessening mental susceptibility, makes it more difficult to arouse the moral nature."[24]

The brain's frontal lobe (where all our decisions are made) is a kind of computer server where thought and emotions "happen."[25] At this point, about an inch behind our forehead, the Holy Spirit accesses human beings. This surely is an advertisement for the distinctiveness and purpose of the Adventist emphasis on health principles!

This interaction, this intersecting of the Holy Spirit with the mind of responsible men and women, has been vastly unappreciated. It was this interaction with the Spirit that helped Jesus to increase "in wisdom and stature, and in favor with God and men" (Luke 2:52). And the promise is ours as well: "And the grace that He received is for us."[26]

Our task is to keep our frontal lobes fresh with pure blood, flooded with plenty of oxygen (daily exercise) and nutrition (a careful diet). Further, our thought processes should guard the avenues to the brain, the avenues of sight, feeling, and touch. Why? So much of what we think and do can overload the frontal lobe so that the quiet voice of the Holy Spirit cannot be heard. For without His voice and His energy, we can never expect to be overcomers!

After the close of probation

Before moving on, let's clear up some confusion regarding the Christian's relationship to Jesus and the Holy Spirit after the close of probation and during the seven last plagues. Some believe that when Jesus leaves the sanctuary as our Mediator, God's people will have to "go it alone" during the plagues. This notion has been a special concern for many, leaving them with a frightful lack of assurance that they could "ever make it on their own."

This confusion arises from a misunderstanding of the role of the Holy Spirit—*He never leaves those who ask for His guidance and empowerment.* In other words, there is no connection between Jesus ceasing His work as High Priest and the continuing, abiding presence of the Holy Spirit. God never intends for believers to ever feel that sometime in the future they must "go it alone" just to prove how perfect they are! This notion does not flow from either the Bible or the writings of Ellen White. Those thoughts grow out of a profound misunderstanding of the character of our heavenly Father, as well as a hasty, even careless, reading of sacred materials.

Between now and the return of Jesus, our task is to continue cooperating with the Holy Spirit, joyfully "work[ing] out [our] salvation with fear and trembling" letting God (the Holy Spirit) work in us "both to will and to do for His good pleasure" (Philippians 2:12, 13). Nothing changes after the close of probation. This is how Jesus lived His life and as many God-fearing, God-loving people have done in every generation since Creation.

Take courage from these thoughts:

> Some few in every generation from Adam resisted his every artifice and stood forth as noble representatives of what it was in the power of man to do and to be—Christ working with human efforts, helping man in overcoming the power of Satan. Enoch and Elijah are the correct representatives of what the race might be through faith in Jesus Christ if they chose to be. Satan was greatly disturbed because these noble, holy men stood untainted amid the moral pollution surrounding them, perfected righteous characters, and were accounted worthy for translation to Heaven.[27]

But I hear the question, What about legalism? Whenever we emphasize "grow in grace" (2 Peter 3:18), "overcoming," and "commandment keeping," most will nod in agreement. But still, they hear the charge of "legalism" reverberating in their heads. How does legalism fit into all this emphasis on character transformation as part of the Christian's assurance of salvation? Let's tackle "legalism" in the next chapter.

---

[1] See pp. 51, 68.

[2] See pp. 64, 69.

[3] "The apostle James saw that dangers would arise in presenting the subject of justification by faith, and he labored to show that genuine faith cannot exist without corresponding works. The experience of Abraham is presented. 'Seest thou,' he says, 'how faith wrought with his works, and by works was faith made perfect?' Thus genuine faith does a genuine work in the believer. Faith and obedience bring a solid, valuable experience. There is a belief that is not a saving faith. The word declares that the devils believe and tremble. The so-called faith that does not work by love and purify the soul will not justify any man" (Ellen G. White, *Signs of the Times*, May 19, 1898).

[4] "Paul here refers not so much to the ritual observances of the ceremonial law alone as to the Jewish concept that a man could save himself by meticulously keeping 'the law,' which consisted of moral, ceremonial, and civil precepts. . . . Paul is concerned [in Galatians] only with the moral and ceremonial codes. The civil code apparently did not enter directly into the problem under discussion. The Jews erred in (1) considering that salvation could be attained to by one's own efforts, through compliance with the requirements of 'the law,' and by virtue of a meritorious life in which a surplus of good deeds would cancel out evil deeds; (2) adding to the law, as given by God, a mass of man-made requirements commonly called 'tradition'; and (3) extending, and attempting to enforce, certain features of the ritual and ceremonial provisions of 'the law' beyond the cross, when they expired by limitation. . . . The word 'law' as used by Paul in the book of Galatians, includes both the moral law, or Decalogue, and the ceremonial law. But Paul is not concerned so much with either of these, as such, as he is with the Jewish legal system of righteousness by works, which was based upon them" (*SDA Bible Commentary*, vol. 6, p. 949).

[5] " 'The law was our schoolmaster to bring us unto Christ, that we might be justified by faith.' In this scripture, the Holy Spirit through the apostle is speaking especially of the moral law. The law reveals sin to us, and causes us to feel our need of Christ, and to flee unto Him for pardon and peace by exercising repentance toward God and faith toward our Lord Jesus Christ. . . .

"The law of ten commandments is not to be looked upon as much from the prohibitory side as from the mercy side. . . . To the obedient it is a wall of protection. We behold in it the goodness of God, who by revealing to men the immutable principles of righteousness seeks to shield them from the evils that result from transgression" (Ellen G. White, *Manuscript 23a*, 1896, cited in *SDABC*, vol 6, p. 1110).

[6] "Obedience to God is liberty from the thralldom of sin, deliverance from human passion and impulse. Man may stand conqueror of himself, conqueror of his own inclinations, conqueror of principalities and powers, and of 'the rulers of the darkness of this world,' and of 'spiritual wickedness in high places.' Ephesians 6:12" (Ellen G. White, *The Ministry of Healing*, p. 131).

[7] See Ellen G. White, *Patriarchs and Prophets,* p. 372.

[8] I am indebted to Paul Penno for this interesting analogy.

[9] "It is not so essential to understand the precise particulars in regard to the relation of the two laws. It is of far greater consequence that we know whether we are transgressing the law of God, whether we stand in obedience or disobedience before the holy precepts" (Ellen G. White, Letter 165, 1901, cited in *SDABC,* vol. 6, p. 1110).

[10] The same challenge John Wesley faced throughout his ministry.

[11] *The Great Controversy,* p. 489.

[12] *Signs of the Times,* May 10, 1899.

[13] "The Spirit was to be given as a regenerating agent, and without this the sacrifice of Christ would have been of no avail. . . . It is the Spirit that makes effectual what has been wrought out by the world's Redeemer. It is by the Spirit that the heart is made pure. Through the Spirit the believer becomes a partaker of the divine nature. Christ has given His Spirit as a divine power to overcome all hereditary and cultivated tendencies to evil, and to impress His own character upon His church" (Ellen G. White, *The Desire of Ages,* p. 671).

[14] "The Lord Jesus came to our world, not to reveal what a God could do, but what a man could do, through faith in God's power to help in every emergency. Man is, through faith, to be a partaker in the divine nature, and to overcome every temptation wherewith he is beset. The Lord now demands that every son and daughter of Adam through faith in Jesus Christ, serve Him in human nature which we now have" (Ellen G. White, Manuscript 1, 1892, printed in *The Review and Herald,* June 17, 1976).

[15] Paul emphasized this empowerment in his Ephesian letter: "He would grant you, according to the riches of His glory, to be strengthened with might through His Spirit in the inner man" (3:16).

[16] "Being confident of this very thing, that He who has begun a good work in you will complete it until the day of Jesus Christ" (Philippians 1:6).

[17] Ellen G. White, *Testimonies for the Church,* vol. 2, p. 355. "Character cannot be changed when Jesus comes, nor just as a man is about to die. Character building must be done in this life" (Ellen G. White, *Testimonies to Ministers and Gospel Workers,* p. 430).

[18] Page 147.

[19] Ellen G. White, *Acts of the Apostles,* pp. 482, 483.

[20] "The fear of the Lord prolongs days" (Proverbs 10:28). "The fear of the Lord is to hate evil" (Proverbs 8:13). "The fear of the Lord is the beginning of wisdom" (Proverbs 9:10).

[21] Ellen G. White, *Christ's Object Lessons,* p. 161.

[22] See pp. 51, 84.

[23] Ellen G. White, *The Desire of Ages,* p. 805. "In describing to His disciples the office work of the Holy Spirit, Jesus sought to inspire them with the joy and hope that inspired His own heart. He rejoiced because of the abundant help He had provided for His church. The Holy Spirit was the highest of all gifts that He could solicit from His Father for the exaltation of His people. The Spirit was to be given as a regenerating agent, and without this the sacrifice of Christ would have been of no avail. The power of evil had been strengthening for centuries, and the submission of men to this satanic captivity was amazing. Sin could be resisted and overcome only through the mighty agency of the Third Person of the Godhead, who would come with no modified energy, but in the fullness of divine power. It is the Spirit that makes effectual what has been wrought out by the world's Redeemer. It is by the Spirit that the

heart is made pure. Through the Spirit the believer becomes a partaker of the divine nature. Christ has given His Spirit as a divine power to overcome all hereditary and cultivated tendencies to evil, and to impress His own character upon His church."—Ibid., p. 671.

[24] Ellen G. White, *Education*, p. 209.

[25] "In recent years the artificial division between thoughts and emotion has begun to give way. Anatomical studies reveal extensive connections between those parts of the brain traditionally associated with our emotions, the limbic system in particular, and the frontal lobes. When the frontal lobes are damaged or destroyed, a person's ability to synthesize signals from the environment, assign priorities, or make balanced decisions is impaired. Once the frontal lobes disconnect from the rest of the brain, the limbic system is free to fire its messages of emotion. The control made possible by the frontal-limbic connections is weakened, and behavior becomes erratic and unpredictable. . . . What does become clear is that even tiny changes in the physical, chemical, and electrical state of the brain can lead to significant shifts in behavior."—Richard M. Restak, M.D., *The Brain* (New York: Bantam Books, 1984), p. 152.

"The frontal lobe . . . the most forward portion, the prefrontal fibers, exert an inhibitory control over our actions, bring them into line with social expectations. Injuries to this area may cause offensive, socially unacceptable behaviors. . . . Anatomists as far back as da Vinci noted that the frontal lobes in human beings were dramatically 'overdeveloped' in comparison to the same region in animals, occupying about one third of the cerebral hemispheres. They are crucial to the functioning of mind in a wide variety of ways, and damage or injury can have many consequences. . . . Patricia Goldmen-Rakic, who is an authority on the prefrontal cortex, notes, 'If thinking is the process of using information to make decisions, then the frontal lobe is crucial for thinking. Without the frontal lobes, we're at the mercy of environment. We respond to events without reflection. We are unable to plan for the future. And it is this capacity to plan for the future that distinguishes us from all other species.' "—Richard M. Restak, M.D., *The Mind* (New York: Bantam Books, 1988), pp. 18, 266, 267.

[26] Ellen G. White, *The Desire of Ages*, p. 73.

[27] Ellen G. White, *Review and Herald*, March 3, 1874.

CHAPTER ELEVEN

And What About "Legalism"?

Seventh-day Adventists have defined themselves as Sabbath keepers and heralds of the Advent. We are distinguished by our high regard for the commandments of God. We take Revelation 14:12 and similar scriptures very seriously. The question for every serious Adventist is not *if* we are to be faithful commandment keepers, but *how.*

The answer to that question directly relates to the major theme of this book. If Christians are to "do something," and if Christians are to have the joy of salvation and the "assurance of faith" (Hebrews 11:22) daily, how do we know if we have done enough in order to be assured?

In these pages, we have been observing how Bible writers and others describe the purpose of the gospel—that God is working out His plan to prepare a people to live forever.[1] For that purpose, the gospel comes to us with two hands, and we receive it with two hands: We need the grace of pardon and the grace of power.[2] Both are gifts. Both are exactly what men and women of faith need daily.[3]

Even as we need both hydrogen and oxygen in order to drink water, so men and women of faith need both pardon and power as they walk in a saving relationship with Jesus. Without both, they soon lapse either into legalism or license. Neither legalism or license to do whatever pleases provides the "assurance of salvation" (Hebrews 10:22).

Why, then, the confusion regarding grace, faith, and assurance that permeates the Christian world? Because men and women in all ages, in all places, have devised ways to calm their hearts into thinking that what they "think" or "do" or "feel" would somehow get God's attention and satisfy the requirements for salvation. They seek assurance and security on their own terms! Of course, many have sincerely done all this ignorantly, and God has His own gracious way of dealing mercifully and appropriately with honest seekers, whether early Vikings, Babylonians, Egyptians, Pharisees in Christ's day, contemporary New Agers, or those who have "only believe" as their mantra.

I don't know what is more self-defeating—legalism or license. Both are surely contemporary problems in all churches. But at the moment let's follow Paul's concern for legalism.

On one hand, Paul was troubled (as all Christians should be) by those who "insist on being saved in some way by which they may perform some important work. When they see that there is no way of weaving self into the work, they reject the salvation provided."[4] It seems he described this group in Colossians 2:16, those who focused on their external behavior—with exacting concern for what they ate and drank, for special religious days, false humility, and physical self-denial.

On the other hand, he spoke unambiguously to those who did not practice what they preached—to those who found theological excuses whereby they could be comfortable to be saved in their sins. For example, he wrote to the Colossian church members as "elect of God" but his strong words and dire warnings could not be misunderstood. They may have turned their backs on "fornication, uncleanness, passion, evil desires, and covetousness," but "now you must also put off all these: anger, wrath, malice, blasphemy, filthy language," lying, etc. (3:5-9). They were "good and regular members" from the standpoint of external behavior; but they still had much to do in areas even more important in the eyes of God—their interpersonal (more hidden) behavior and attitudes.

Ellen White clearly delineated these two kinds of church members who had not yet grasped the healing power of the gospel: "those who would be saved by their merits, and those who would be saved in their sins."[5] In a way, both are legalists. They both want salvation without character transformation!

What does legalism mean? So many definitions afflict us. For example, many in the Christian world think that a legalist is one who does not understand the liberation of grace; thus, any attempt to keep God's laws is wrongheaded and simply an example of "righteousness by works." For them, any effort to pattern our lives after our Lord's example is hopelessly impossible and results in legalism.

Another faction, with a slightly different twist, believes that sanctification is not an integral or necessary part of the gospel equation (pardon and power). They think that Paul's overcoming formula (Philippians

2:12, 13)[6] has been misunderstood, or is, at least, misleading. For them, faith is essentially appreciation and acceptance without character transformation because in their limited understanding of the gospel, they say that we can do nothing to add to what Christ "did" on the cross. Anything that we think we should "do" is thus legalism at work. "Perfection," for them, should be dropped from the Christian's vocabulary![7]

The Adventist Church emphasizes that men and women of faith joyfully comply with the Ten Commandments (and anything else that comes to them as "light") as their part in the divine-human co-op program—without which salvation would not happen! And some have accused this emphasis as legalism! So, because of this withering charge, the sense of assurance, for some, becomes unsettled.

Ellen White has described various forms of legalism in contrast to commandment keepers who, in genuine faith, rely fully on God to "will and do for His good pleasure" in their lives:

> All legalism . . . [does not] have a proper estimate of sin.[8]

> Legalists, like the priests and rulers in Christ's day were "fixed in a rut of ceremonialism . . . satisfied with a legal religion . . . made up of ceremonies and the injunctions of men."[9]

> A legalist who "is trying to reach heaven by his own works in keeping the law is attempting an impossibility. There is no safety for one who has merely a legal religion, a form of godliness."[10]

> A legal religion can never lead souls to Christ; for it is a loveless, Christless religion. . . . The round of religious ceremonies, the external humiliation, the imposing sacrifice, proclaim that the doer of these things regards himself as righteous, and as entitled to heaven; but it is all a deception.[11]

> Icy hearts hav[ing] only a legal religion.[12]

> Legalists "go crippling along, dwarfed in religious growth, because they have in their ministry a legal religion. The power of the grace of God is not felt to be a living, effectual necessity, an abiding principle."[13]

> The spirit of bondage is engendered by seeking to live in accordance with legal religion, through striving to fulfill the claims of the law in our own strength.[14]

A legal religion is insufficient to bring the soul into harmony with God. The hard, rigid orthodoxy of the Pharisees, destitute of contrition, tenderness, or love, was only a stumbling block to sinners.[15]

Legal religion will not answer for this age. We may perform all the outward acts of service, and yet be as destitute of the quickening influence of the Holy Spirit as the hills of Gilboa were destitute of dew and rain.[16]

In summary, a legalist has the words but not the music! He sees the importance of obedience; he flees from license—from pushing the envelope to the extremes. In a way, legalists get satisfaction out of punishing themselves into "being good"—precisely what Paul calls the "yoke of bondage" that he applies to all commandment keepers who are trying their best to be good without the "power of the grace of God." They enjoy only a crippled, dwarfed Christian experience. They need to hear the fullness of the gospel!

As C. S. Lewis put it, some think "that God wanted simply obedience to a set of rules; whereas He really wants people of a particular sort."[17]

This whole subject of legalism, the relation between grace and faith, between gospel and law, between Christ as Savior and Christ as Lord, was on display at the General Conference in Minneapolis in 1888. I have never seen it better put than in the following words—words written to help clarify the 1888 issues:

Let this point be fully settled in every mind: If we accept Christ as a Redeemer, we must accept Him as a Ruler. We cannot have the assurance and perfect confiding trust in Christ as our Savior until we acknowledge Him as our King and are obedient to His commandments. Thus we evidence our allegiance to God. We have then the genuine ring in our faith, for it is a working faith. It works by love.[18]

Here is one clear clue as to how "assurance of faith" is found. The issues of the 1888 Conference should be understood. Clarity on these issues will greatly simplify and strengthen our personal response to God's call for a special people with a special message for a special time. The speakers at the Minneapolis Conference nailed legalism to the wall (as they did also in following years), and it should never have been a problem ever again—but it keeps getting down off the wall![19]

Speakers at the 1888 Conference went further back than the Protestant Reformation in opening up the purpose of the gospel more completely. The Adventist Church, as well as the rest of the world, needs to hear what was said at that conference.

What was happening within the Seventh-day Adventist Church during the 1880s that brought these core issues to a head? Many references describe the Adventist Church during the 1880s in bleak terms.

Admittedly, Adventists were sticklers to the commandments; they could debate down anybody regarding the immutability of the Ten Commandments and the continuing authority of the Sabbath commandment.

But many were blind to Ellen White's charge that they were Laodiceans, virtually legalists. This lukewarm Laodicean condition was partly due to the focus on the Sabbath truth and the soon return of Jesus, while *assuming* that justification by faith was a given. Unconsciously, "keeping the commandments" eventually became the same as "the faith of Jesus" and "loving God." This silent shift eroded Christian experience, beclouded an intimate personal relationship with Jesus, and set the stage for Ellen White's charge that their religion was as dry as the "hills of Gilboa."[20]

In the early 1880s Ellen White spoke to Adventist ministers: "Too often this truth is presented in cold theory. . . . A theory of the truth without vital godliness cannot remove the moral darkness which envelops the soul."[21]

Our church, generally, had drifted into a legalistic experience, holding fast to their commandment keeping. But a rich, Spirit-filled life— a heart religion—that moves people from one victory over sin to another, from self-centeredness to a generous, loving person, was sadly lacking.

Consequently, the world had not been given a fair picture of what the messages of the three angels (Revelation 14) were meant to be. Therefore, the great need for a re-emphasis of the "everlasting gospel" within the setting of 1888:

> The message [brought by A. T. Jones and E. J. Waggoner]
> of the gospel of His grace was to be given to the church in
> clear and distinct lines, that the world should no longer say
> that Seventh-day Adventists talk the law, the law, but do not
> teach or believe Christ.[22]

What follows may be the most informed description of the 1888 focus on the Adventist message:

The Lord in His great mercy sent a most precious message to His people through Elders Waggoner and Jones. This message was to bring more prominently before the world the uplifted Savior, the sacrifice for the sins of the whole world. It presented justification through faith in the Surety; it invited the people to receive the righteousness of Christ, which is made manifest in obedience to all the commandments of God. Many had lost sight of Jesus. They needed to have their eyes directed to His divine person, His merits, and His changeless love for the human family. All power is given into His hands, that He may dispense rich gifts unto men, imparting the priceless gift of His own righteousness to the helpless human agent. This is the message that God commanded to be given to the world. It is the third angel's message, which is to be proclaimed with a loud voice, and attended with the outpouring of His Spirit in a large measure.[23]

That is a remarkable paragraph! In that paragraph we have the distinctive message of the Seventh-day Adventist Church regarding righteousness by faith; here also we see why the emphasis of 1888 was light years ahead of our illustrious Protestant Reformers. This is a layer of solid granite on which we may safely rest our "assurance of faith."

That paragraph summarizes in different words the purpose of the gospel and God's plan for placing the universe on a secure basis.[24] It sets forth the relationship of justification (setting right) and sanctification (keeping right) within the "righteousness of Christ which is made manifest in obedience to all the commandments of God." These "priceless gifts" were pardon and power to "the helpless human agent." Is there any other church with this clear mission statement? Apparently, it is the core of the "loud" cry that will be "attended with the outpouring of His Spirit."

The 1888 messages not only nailed legalism to the wall; they opened up the floodgates of joy for those who received them.

The point I am making here is that the coldness of nineteenth-century orthodoxy (primarily concern for doctrinal correctness) that prevailed generally in conservative Protestantism had overcome zealous Adventists. The result: "too many Christless sermons preached." Legalism prevailed! Assurance of salvation rested on external conformity to the law (which, of course, can be measured and ticked off the checklist, providing a presumptuous assurance of salvation).

When legalism prevails, either self-righteousness and pride or discouragement and spiritual depression soon follow. Intent on being

Christians, legalists (most often unknowingly) see only rigor, demand, and checklists. Jesus as their personal Savior, their personal Enabler, their closest Friend, as faithful High Priest, becomes obscured under the weight of one demand after another. Duty is not a delight—just one more step to climb. Though such church members desire to please God, they feel the stress and see only the cloud.[25]

Those who do keep up their courage believe they must try harder, thinking that is the way to find peace and assurance. (Here again is a good example of not understanding the full meaning of "faith" and how to "trust in God's faithfulness."[26]) Unconsciously, they become more focused on lawkeeping than on the Christ of the law. How would they do that? By becoming even more circumspect in their business dealings, in their Sabbath keeping, in being even more careful about their dress, in their TV watching, and whatever else. But, burdened with that misunderstanding of faith and assurance, no wonder people never feel that they have done "enough."

All this emphasis on loyalty to the law is most commendable in our day of unbridled license when moral standards seem to have evaporated.[27] But there is no joy in simply trying harder—no matter how much approval one may be getting from others! However, more rigor— even more time devoted to Bible study and prayer—is not the answer to the joyless but disciplined, perhaps even, proud, heart of a legalist!

The answer to cold legalism was clearly presented in the "precious message" that Elders Jones and Waggoner and Ellen White brought to the 1888 General Conference and in various books and sermons after that momentous conference. That message was not a "get-ready-or-else" threat, but tremendous good news as to how to live the Christian life and prepare to live forever. The messages restored Jesus as One who was very "near" to His people, near even before sinners realized the Godhead's love for them. He was seen as One who, in His human nature, completely identified with fallen men and women.[28] And as One who showed us how we may become conquerors over sin. His role as our High Priest was given a clear focus in the 1888 messages as a vital element in helping us to overcome our sins as we help to close the great controversy.

The golden thread of this "good news" (to which Ellen White, in response, said, "Every fiber of my heart said, 'Amen' "[29]) links these thoughts: Our standing with God does not depend upon our rigor or even our initiative in claiming His promises, but on our willingness to receive what He has already provided—and that He will continue to provide salvation for us, if we do not frustrate His will.[30] That thought stands legalism on its head!

A haunting warning hangs over all of us today as we relate to this "precious message" that remains perennially relevant:

> I have no smooth message to bear to those who have been so long as false guideposts, pointing the wrong way. If you reject Christ's delegated messengers, you reject Christ. Neglect this great salvation, kept before you for years, despise this glorious offer of justification through the blood of Christ and sanctification through the cleansing power of the Holy Spirit, and there remaineth no more sacrifice for sins, but a certain fearful looking for of judgment and fiery indignation.[31]

I ask, after reading that paragraph, could our understanding regarding the elements of righteousness by faith and the assurance of faith be made any clearer?

Some say, with plenty of reasons, that our problem in the Adventist Church today is not legalism but rampant license. Perhaps! But the sly, subtle, ever-present inclination toward legalism resides as a virus in every religious body—corporately and individually—ready to multiply into open disease unless the immune system is kept healthy. Especially is this virus alive within those who try to impress God with their "commandment keeping"!

The virus of legalism saps the enthusiasm and vitality of a dedicated Christian, even when performing the noble virtues of Christianity. The virus provides the words, but not the music; somehow, for the legalist, "doing" religion overshadows "being" religious! The following counsel is most helpful to all of us:

> Some who come to God by repentance and confession, and even believe that their sins are forgiven, still fail of claiming, as they should, the promises of God. They do not see that Jesus is an ever-present Savior; and they are not ready to commit the keeping of their souls to Him, relying upon Him to perfect the work of grace begun in their hearts. While they think they are committing themselves to God, there is a great deal of self-dependence. There are conscientious souls that trust partly to God and partly to themselves. They do not look to God, to be kept by His power, but depend upon watchfulness against temptation and the performance of certain duties for acceptance with Him. There are no victories in this kind of faith. Such persons toil to no purpose; their souls are in continual bondage, and they find no rest until their burdens are laid at the feet of Jesus.

There is need of constant watchfulness and of earnest, loving devotion, but these will come naturally when the soul is kept by the power of God through faith. We can do nothing, absolutely nothing, to commend ourselves to divine favor. We must not trust at all to ourselves or to our good works; but when as erring, sinful beings we come to Christ, we may find rest in His love. God will accept every one that comes to Him trusting wholly in the merits of a crucified Savior. Love springs up in the heart. There may be no ecstasy of feeling, but there is an abiding, peaceful trust. Every burden is light; for the yoke which Christ imposes is easy. Duty becomes a delight, and sacrifice a pleasure. The path that before seemed shrouded in darkness becomes bright with beams from the Sun of Righteousness. This is walking in the light as Christ is in the light.[32]

So let's get practical. For example: Adventists with their special emphasis on health principles, especially should ask themselves: Why am I a vegetarian? Why do I avoid tobacco and alcoholic beverages, even caffeine products? Is it primarily a sense of demand—"I must be a faithful health reformer to gain God's approval"?

The answer is "Yes" and "No."

No, in the sense that God already has reconciled Himself to you (see 2 Corinthians 5:18, 19)—therefore, all the good, and all the bad, you do will not change His love for you.

No, in the sense that the purpose of health reform is not primarily to please God; He gave us the health message as all parents give their children counsel. Parents give counsel because they love their children and want to see them avoid terrible mistakes. When children take advice readily, obviously their parents are happy and approve what they are doing.

Yes, God does love us unconditionally. No, God does not approve what we do unconditionally. God is not happy to see us destroy ourselves or even to diminish our potential.

The one question that may help all of us to think carefully about the cloud of legalism is this: Am I keeping the Sabbath carefully, paying tithe faithfully, and giving Bible studies diligently *to impress God or to honor Him?* The answer may take some thought. The question needs to be asked every day. It is so easy to slip into legalism!

Remember our Lord's warning regarding the Pharisees? " 'Unless your righteousness exceeds the righteousness of the scribes and Pharisees, you will by no means enter the kingdom of heaven' " (Matthew 5:20).

What was wrong with these commandment-keeping, health-reform-ing, tithe-paying church members (who eventually murdered Jesus)? They had a "legal religion." To put it bluntly:

All their pretensions of piety, their human inventions and ceremonies, and even their boasted performance of the out-ward requirements of the law, could not avail to make them holy. They were not pure in heart or noble and Christlike in character.

A legal religion is insufficient to bring the soul into har-mony with God. The hard, rigid orthodoxy of the Pharisees, destitute of contrition, tenderness, or love, was only a stum-bling block to sinners. They were like the salt that had lost its savor; for their influence had no power to preserve the world from corruption.[33]

But there is another angle—we should not accuse all legalists of being too proud to seek forgiveness, too proud to be repentant. Many thrive on repeated moments of repentance, on rising and falling, sin-ning and seeking forgiveness, as if that were all they could expect this side of heaven.[34]

The danger is that legalists (unless they finally see the fullness of the gospel) do not go on in their Christian growth, reaching out con-stantly for "moral renovation and the necessity of divine enlighten-ment. . . . Christ presented their [Pharisees] religion as devoid of saving faith. There are many who will be lost, because they depend on legal religion, or mere repentance for sin. But repentance for sin alone cannot work the salvation of any soul. Man cannot be saved by his own works. Without Christ it is impossible for him to render perfect obedience to the law of God; and heaven can never be gained by an imperfect obedience; for this would place all heaven in jeopardy, and make possible a second rebellion."[35]

However, we all should beware of pointing the finger at legalists. Why? Because "the spirit of Pharisaism is the spirit of human na-ture."[36] How many are guilt-free from doing religious things and hop-ing to have others notice our good works, our wonderful intentions?

The problem is that "careful" commandment keeping, on one hand, and "good work" for the sick, the homeless, the handicapped, etc., on the other, may not spring from the purest motive. Both groups may operate from self-centered motives, often unknowingly.

But there is another group—the struggling Christian with the right motive, who may be living in legalistic gloom. Sad! They need to hear *all* the good news! Obviously, they shouldn't relax their commandment keeping; but they do need to take the hand of Him who provides the inner strength to be joyfully obedient to His Father's will. They need to see God as their Friend, not as their severe taskmaster. They need to hang their helpless souls on their great Friend who never lets go! They need to fall often into their Lord's everlasting arms (where forgiveness is His nature) whenever they don't measure up to His gracious, loving example. He does not condemn us for our sins but for our reluctance to keep walking into the light we all have (John 3:17-21). He is always there to help us get up and to keep walking.

Over the years these "faithful" church members have given their best to the church—but not with much joy! Think of it, for more than a century a good percentage of Adventist tithes and offerings have come from the pockets of those whom others have called legalists! In contrast were church members who have wanted the "blessing" of Christianity without the responsibility of genuine faith—obedience.[37]

Both groups need to hear the fullness of the gospel! Both groups need to hear the Lord say: "I know you for what you are and for what you want to be!" Both groups need to have genuine assurance today! Both groups will melt under the radiant sunshine of joy and peace when they understand how eagerly Jesus wants to give them assurance today that He will walk them all the way into the kingdom.

Both groups need to hear daily that their "hope is not in [themselves]; it is in Christ. Your weakness is united to His strength, your ignorance to His wisdom, your frailty to His enduring might."[38]

---

[1] See pp. 51, 68.

[2] See pp. 19, 58, 69.

[3] "Another lesson the tabernacle, through its service of sacrifice, was to teach—the lesson of pardon of sin, and power through the Savior for obedience unto life" (*Education*, p. 36).

[4] Ellen G. White, *The Desire of Ages*, p. 280.

[5] *The Great Controversy*, p. 572.

[6] See pp 80, 83, 84.

[7] For Adventists to think this way, they would have to repudiate the binding authority of the fourth commandment as well as all the others. The only moral restraint would be the laws of one's community or those self-imposed.

[8] *Signs of the Times*, April 9, 1894.

[9] *Acts of the Apostles*, p. 15.

[10] *The Desire of Ages*, p. 172.

[11] Ibid., p. 280.

[12] *Selected Messages*, bk. 3, p. 177.

[13] Ibid., bk. 3, p. 189.

[14] *The Youth's Instructor*, September 22, 1892, cited in *SDABC* vol. 6, p. 1077.

[15] *Thoughts From the Mount of Blessing*, p. 53.

[16] *Testimonies for the Church*, vol. 6, pp. 417, 418.

[17] Lewis, *Mere Christianity* (San Francisco, Calif: HarperCollins Publisher, 2001), p. 80.

[18] Ellen G. White, *Faith and Works*, p. 16.

[19] In 1888, the essence of the messages brought by Elders A. T. Jones and E. J. Waggoner and Ellen White recovered lost or compromised biblical truths. It was not merely a recovery of Protestant Reformation theology. Hardly! No Reformer could be used as a reference, then or today. However, the Reformers did agree on the Protestant principle that rejected the papal principle of church authority over biblical authority, opening up the world to a different way of listening to truth. For their courage and clear thinking we will always be in their debt.

[20] *Testimonies*, vol. 6, p. 417; "As a people, we have preached the law until we are as dry as the hills of Gilboa that had neither dew nor rain. We must preach Christ in the law, and there will be sap and nourishment in the preaching that will be as food to the famishing flock of God. We must not trust in our own merits at all, but in the merits of Jesus of Nazareth. Our eyes must be anointed with eye-salve" (*Review and Herald*, March 11, 1890).

[21] Ibid., vol. 4, pp. 313, 314.

[22] Ellen G. White, *Testimonies to Ministers and Gospel Workers*, p. 92.

[23] Ibid., pp. 91, 92.

[24] See *The Desire of Ages*, p. 759.

[25] See letter in the first chapter.

[26] See pp. 52–61.

[27] Robert H. Bork's *Slouching Towards Gomorrah* (New York, N.Y.: Reganbooks, HarperCollins Publisher, 1996) is one of many current books deploring the moral slippage of "modern liberalism and American decline."

[28] See *The Desire of Ages*, p. 49.

[29] *The Ellen G. White 1888 Materials*, vol. 1, p. 349.

[30] Ellen G. White, *Steps to Christ*, pp, 27, 34; *Thoughts From the Mount of Blessing*, pp.76, 139; *The Desire of Ages*, pp. 176, 483.

[31] Ellen G. White, *Testimonies to Ministers and Gospel Workers*, pp. 97, 98.

[32] Ellen G. White, *Faith and Works*, pp. 38, 39.

[33] Ellen G. White, *Thoughts From the Mount of Blessing*, p. 53

[34] "Are there those here who have been sinning and repenting, sinning and repenting, and will they continue to do so till Christ shall come? May God help us that we may be truly united to Christ, the living vine, and bear fruit to the glory of God!" (Ellen G. White, *Review and Herald*, April 21, 1891).

[35] Ellen G. White, *Signs of the Times*, December 30, 1889.

[36] Ellen G. White, *Thoughts From the Mount of Blessing*, p. 79.

[37] "They extol the riches of free grace, and attempt to cover themselves with an appearance of righteousness, hoping to screen their defects of character; but their efforts will be of no avail in the day of God" (Ellen G. White, *Christ's Object Lessons*, p. 316).

[38] Ellen G. White, *Steps to Christ*, p. 70.

CHAPTER TWELVE

Also, What About That "Wedding Garment"?

Whenever one focuses on assurance *now,* another subject pops up. The Bible talks about the "wedding garment" that the redeemed will wear (Matthew 22:1-14; Ephesians 5:26, 27). In fact, John the revelator wrote that our Lord's bride (the redeemed) will wear this garment— "in fine linen, clean and bright, for the fine linen is the righteous acts of the saints" (Revelation 19:8).

Those who are troubled about "works righteousness" have difficulty with this text. The usual explanation is that this garment is really the robe of Christ's righteousness imputed to all believers. They go on to say that any attempt to make this "robe" into anything that a Christian must "do" is pure legalism and not the message of grace. Further, they say, if one focuses on the "righteous deeds of the saints," how could he have any "assurance" of salvation *now?*

What shall we make of these two stark differences, both looking at the same biblical texts?

Let's remember that the ultimate purpose of the gospel is to prepare a people who can be trusted with eternal life.[1] When we recognize that the good news provides both pardon and power in God's plan to restore in us His "image," it should seem easier to figure out how the "robe" and wedding garment is acquired. But let's review how everything we have learned so far helps us to answer those who may be confused regarding certain biblical statements.

In Matthew 22:1-14 Jesus gave the parable of the wedding feast. The high point of the parable focuses on the king greeting the wedding guests. But the king discovers " 'a man there who did not have on a wedding garment' " (verse 11). Bad news—he was punished irrevocably!

Now, what shall we make of this parable? Jesus did not elaborate. However, I have found insights in Ellen White's exposition of this parable that parallel the New Testament teaching of the full gospel.

We are told that "the parable . . . opens before us a lesson of the highest consequence" and that "the wedding garment represents the character which all must possess who shall be accounted fit guests for the wedding."[2]

How do men and women acquire this wedding garment? "The fine linen, says the Scripture (Revelation 19:8) is 'the righteousness of the saints.' It is the righteousness of Christ, His own unblemished character that through faith is imparted to all who receive Him as their personal Savior. . . . Christ in His humanity wrought out a perfect character, and this character He offers to impart to us."[3]

Here we have in parable form the outline of "righteousness by faith," that is, how righteousness is acquired by faith. Men and women of faith, from the first repenting moment, through many repenting moments thereafter, have cooperated with the Holy Spirit as He reproduces the character of Christ in them.[4] Their part in character development is to cooperate with God who is willing to do His good pleasure in men and women of faith.

The developing character that is reflecting Jesus more and more is not a product of "human devising." Any man or woman of faith knows that all too well. The most we can do is to keep our eye single, not double-minded, trusting in His promises that He will "complete" the good work that He began (see Philippians 1:6). The new covenant experience reflects a character development void of "human devising" because it grows out of the Lord's promise to " 'put My laws into their hearts, and in their minds I will write them' " (Hebrews 10:16).

This character transformation is another way of describing "what it means to be clothed with the garment of His righteousness."[5] Here again Ellen White sheds light on the meaning of "righteousness":

> Righteousness is right-doing, and it is by their deeds that all will be judged. Our characters are revealed by what we do. The works show whether the faith is genuine. . . . Whatever our profession, it amounts to nothing unless Christ is revealed in works of righteousness.[6]

We are dealing with metaphors when we talk about "garments" and "robes." What we are really talking about is character transformation which is surely a gift, but a gift that is imparted, not only imputed.[7]

> Those who reject the gift of Christ's righteousness are rejecting the attributes of character which would constitute them the sons and daughters of God. They are rejecting that which alone could give them a fitness for a place at the marriage feast. . . . It is in this life that we are to put on the robe of Christ's righteousness. This is our only opportunity to form characters for the home which Christ has made ready for those who obey His commandments.[8]

Powerful parable that embraces all aspects of the everlasting gospel!

Closely linked to this wedding parable is the dramatic, full-color, preview of the real wedding for which the whole universe is waiting—the marriage of the Lamb!

When men and women of faith walk into the "marriage of the Lamb" they walk in as His bride! But notice how John carefully chose his words: the bride, the Lamb's wife " 'has *made herself* ready' " (Revelation 19:7, emphasis supplied).

How did she make herself "ready"? (After all, no bridegroom makes his bride ready for her wedding! The bride has preparation to do that no bridegroom can do for her.)

What was her preparation that no one else could do? John tells us that the bride finally comes to the altar after leaving the Bridegroom waiting at the altar for a long, long time. She comes "arrayed in fine linen, clean and bright, for the fine linen is the righteous acts[9] of the saints" (Revelation 19:8). This picture is enough to take our breath away.

Men and women of faith, symbolized by the bride, are at the wedding because the Bridegroom "can trust them."[10] The bride has demonstrated her wholehearted appreciation for His gift of love and all that comes with it. She can offer the Bridegroom only her purity and her track record (her "righteous acts") for the Bridegroom to trust her forever!

This wedding has been on God's heart for a long, long time. This is His reward for taking the risk of making men and women as part of His plan to settle the great controversy. They have settled the question as to whether sinful men and women could ever freely reverse their rebel ways, by the grace of God, and be restored to a life that truly reflects their Maker.

We have discovered through these pages that "Satan had claimed that it was impossible for man to obey God's commandments; and in our own strength it is true that we cannot obey them. . . . [But] when a soul receives Christ, he receives power to live the life of Christ."[11] And when that restored life becomes a forever habit pattern, "they have a right to join the blood-washed throng."[12]

Men and women of faith will one day have the "right" (by the empowering grace of God) to live forever! Potent words! Why? God can "trust" them! Why? "Character . . . decides destiny"[13] and that has been the whole purpose of the gospel—of why Christ came to earth and died. Such men and women of faith help to place the universe "on an eternal basis of security."[14]

And what will the universe say about God's risk and His judgment regarding the redeemed? Listen to the chorus echoing from world to world: " 'Alleluia! Salvation and glory and honor and power to the Lord our God! For true and righteous are His judgments' " (Revelation 19:1, 2; see also Revelation 15:3).

All this reality on the horizon today should give men and women of faith plenty of hope. But more—knowing that the Lord at the end of the road is the One who is walking beside us today should give us present assurance of salvation.

No mystery about who wears the robe of Christ's righteousness! Wearing the robe today means that we are "abiding in Him" *today!* Wearing the robe means that we are choosing to walk *today* "just as He walked" (1 John 2:6). Wearing the robe means that we are saying "Yes" to whatever light the Holy Spirit is shining on our paths *today.*

All this adds up to our grateful thanks for this present "assurance of faith" (Hebrews 10:22).

But, there remains that lingering worry: This sounds almost too good to be true! It sounds too much like "perfectionism"— and that's scary! How can we understand the difference between "perfectionism" and possessing the "right to join the blood-washed throng"?

---

[1] See pp. 51, 68.

[2] *Christ's Object Lessons,* p. 307.

[3] Ibid., pp. 310, 311.

[4] See *The Desire of Ages,* p. 805.

[5] "When we submit ourselves to Christ, the heart is united with His heart, the will is merged in His will, the mind becomes one with His mind, the thoughts are brought into captivity to Him; we live His life. This is what it means to be clothed with the garment of His righteousness" (Ellen G. White, *Christ's Object Lessons,* p. 312).

[6] Ibid., pp. 312, 313.

[7] Some may say that Zechariah 3 tells us something much different regarding

the believer's "robe." Not really. The wonderful good news is that Jesus can outshine Satan's accusations with the bright light of the Cross, that no person who repents needs to carry the burden of guilt. Christ imputes His righteousness, not to cover the believer's "filthy garments," but to "take away the filthy garments." Genuine faith is penitent when it asks for pardon, and that is why "the Angel of the Lord" admonished forgiven Joshua as to how to walk in his new freedom: " ' "If you will walk in My ways, and if you will keep My command, then you shall also judge My house, and likewise have charge of My courts; I will give you places to walk among these who stand here" ' " (Zechariah 3:1-7). "As Joshua pleaded before the Angel, so the remnant church, with brokenness of heart and unfaltering faith, will plead for pardon and deliverance through Jesus, their Advocate. . . . The assaults of Satan are strong, his delusions are subtle; but the Lord's eye is upon His people. Their affliction is great, the flames of the furnace seem about to consume them; but Jesus will bring them forth as gold tried in the fire. Their earthliness will be removed, that through them the image of Christ may be perfectly revealed. . . . He does not leave His people to be overcome by Satan's temptations. . . . To those who call upon Him for strength for the development of Christian character, He will give all needed help" (Ellen G. White, *Prophets and Kings*, pp. 588–590; see *SDABC*, vol. 5, p. 480).

[8] Ellen G. White, *Christ's Object Lessons*, pp. 316, 317, 319. "The people of God must cleave to God, else they will lose their bearings. If they cherish hereditary and cultivated traits of character that misrepresent Christ, while professedly His disciples, they are represented by the man coming to the gospel feast without having on the wedding garment, and by the foolish virgins which had no oil in their vessels with their lamps. We must cleave to that which God pronounces to be truth, though the whole world may be arrayed against it" (Manuscript 140, 1901 cited in *SDABC* vol. 4, p. 189).

[9] *Dikaiomata*, "righteous deeds." Here the focus is on the life practice of "righteous" men and women of faith, the sanctified product of Christians empowered by the Holy Spirit.

[10] Ellen G. White, *Christ's Object Lessons*, p. 315.

[11] Ibid., p. 314.

[12] Ibid., p. 315.

[13] Ibid., pp. 74, 84, 123, 260, 264, 270, 310, 356, 365, 378, 388.

[14] Ellen G. White, *The Desire of Ages*, p. 759.

CHAPTER THIRTEEN

Perfection–the Relentless Pursuit

I remember those many weeks in 1993 when I thought I would never walk again without a cane, or perhaps a walker. After two surgeries for herniated discs (the surgeon said, "exploded"), I needed much time with Phil Stoddard, an expert, empathetic physical therapist in Auburn, California. We inched along, reducing pain and stretching for lost strength in my strangely numb, but painful right leg.

On Phil's wall is a poster, a Nike ad: "There is no finish line." Three times a week, for months, I contemplated that message. It fit exactly a chapter in a book I was completing at that time, on the books of Philippians and Colossians.[1]

That motto became Paul's message from the day he met Jesus face to face on the road to Damascus until he was beheaded in Rome, action-packed years later. It became his memorable counsel in Philippians:

> Not that I have already attained, or am already perfected; but I press on, that I may lay hold of that for which Christ Jesus has also laid hold of me. Brethren, I do not count myself to have apprehended; but one thing I do, forgetting those things which are behind and reaching forward to those things which are ahead, I press toward the goal for the prize of the upward call of God in Christ Jesus (3:12-14).

Before Damascus Paul thought he had it all—wrapped up in prestige and power. In a way, he had the future wrapped up—totally secure with (1) the approval of the highest religious leaders, and (2) his spiritual assurance that he was a member of the spiritual elite.

After Damascus, Paul realized that he had been resting for years in presumptuous assurance. Even his friends had considered him "blameless" (Philippians 3:6)! But after meeting Jesus as his new Friend, Paul's spiritual world turned upside down. He shifted from the security of righteousness gained by conforming to legal requirements to the "surpassing worth of knowing Christ Jesus my Lord" (3:8, RSV).

I read somewhere that driving at a speed of thirty miles an hour one can absorb only seven words from a billboard. People pay big money to catch my attention—with only a few words.

The same goes for bumper stickers. Some make sense; some you wish you had not read! Sometimes we have to get very close to get the point, such as the one that read: "The main thing is to keep the main thing the main thing."

Paul's "main thing" after Damascus was to do "one thing . . . forgetting what lies behind and straining forward to what lies ahead, I press on toward the goal for the prize of the upward call of God in Christ Jesus" (Philippians 3:13, 14, RSV). What did Paul mean? So much misunderstanding has occurred through the centuries as to what Paul meant, *and those misunderstandings directly affect one's understanding of Christian assurance and that troubling word,* perfection.

- Paul is reemphasizing our Lord's harvest principle (see Mark 4; Revelation 14:14-16), which interlaces his many letters.[2] We plant hard, dry corn seeds, and then we nurture them to "press on" toward the goal for which they were planted. Perfect corn seeds are expected to mature, to produce a harvest—if they do not keep growing, they cease to be "perfect." Plants that stop growing do not reach "the goal, the prize." They may have started well, but they missed the point of how to remain perfect in the eyes of their planters.[3]
- Paul is passing out an open secret of happy Christians: Forget the past! But that may be easier said than done.

The Greek word we translate as "forgetting" is an ancient athletic term that describes a runner who surpasses another. The athlete knows that he must not be distracted by looking back over his shoulders—he must keep his eyes on the prize ahead. The Greek term is intensive—*don't keep looking over your shoulder!*

Growing Christians believe their Forever Friend—the past has been forgiven, if it has been confessed and forsaken (Proverbs 28:13; 1 John

1:9). The load is gone; maybe not forgotten, but forgiven. And they know that their Forever Friend is helping them to redirect those neural paths that led them into those moral quagmires.[4]

Paul is also asking us to forget those spiritual crutches that we once used to impress God. Forget the notion that we are good because we are not really bad! Forget the idea that we can be Christians without knowing, in a trusting, experiential way, Jesus as our personal Savior from sin!

- Paul reminds us that this focus on pressing on "toward the goal for the prize of the upward call" is not a once-a-week affair—only when we are in church, for example.

The Greek word translated "press" depicts a runner or a chariot racer who leans into the race, stretching every muscle, never giving up, keeping his eye on his prize. The word is similar in meaning to other words we have used in previous chapters, such as "strive" and "abide." After meeting Jesus, Paul formed a life habit of leaning into the future, with his eyes zoomed in on his goal—honoring God, doing His service. For Paul there was "no finish line."

- Paul's emphasis is on direction, not perfection. Perfection is a word that must be used carefully because of its rampant abuse. We could present the gospel and the whole intent of the Bible without using this English word.

When Jesus and others used the Greek word we translate as "perfect," and "perfection," they are not referring to a state or level in which a person is beyond temptation or beyond the possibility of sin—any more than Jesus (a perfect Person) was beyond temptation. Neither does the Bible mean that perfection demands a level of physical and mental accomplishments in which no illnesses arise or no mental mistakes (such as in mathematics) are made.

For the Greek word often translated "perfection," many English translations interchange such terms as "maturity" or "completeness." But what does biblical perfection or maturity or completeness mean? Those words sound ominous, even scary.

I know that when some people see that word *perfection* something tends to freeze up. Emotions take over. God's promises and Christ's support system seem to get blurred. Why? For two reasons: (1) Most of us are well aware of our deficiencies, and (2) we don't see very many "perfect" people.

Consequently, we try to slide over those biblical texts that clearly hold up the Christian's goal of perfection.[5] And we discount Ellen White's emphasis on perfection.

But what are the Bible and Ellen White really saying about "perfection"? First of all, they are not working from Greek, philosophical definitions such as absolute perfection, beyond which there is no need to grow mentally, physically, emotionally, etc. Hardly! Their concern is "moral perfection."

Before and after Ellen White's statement that "moral perfection is required of all," she provides her context that few read. I think Ellen White explains this subject as well as anyone I have ever read:

> The Lord chooses His own agents, and each day under different circumstances He gives them a trial in His plan of operation. In each true-hearted endeavor to work out His plan, He chooses His agents not because they are perfect but because, through a connection with Him, they may gain perfection.
>
> God will accept only those who are determined to aim high. He places every human agent under obligation to do his best. *Moral perfection is required of all.* Never should we lower the standard of righteousness in order to accommodate inherited or cultivated tendencies to wrong-doing.[6]

In other words, God is in charge of "perfecting" His people. He is looking for people who want to cooperate with Him and who will let the purpose of the gospel be worked out in their lives. All He wants from us is our (1) willingness to stay connected with Him, (2) our determination to aim high in all aspects of our lives, and (3) our integrity in honoring His high standards.

Maybe the makers of the Lexus automobile have discovered the truth about the big picture that most theologians have missed. Lexus manufacturers are committed to "the relentless pursuit of perfection." Like the apostle Paul, they never think that they have "arrived" (Philippians 3:12). They are relentlessly pursuing the "perfect" car. They will continue to aim high, never lowering their standards.

Doesn't that sound like the program we all will be on in the new earth? Always pursuing the goal of Christlikeness! Forever learning how to be more gracious, more considerate, more capable of explaining the plan of salvation to others on worlds afar!

One thought that should seem obvious! In our "relentless pursuit" of "moral perfection," we should always be aware that it is impossible to say, "We have reached our goal!" Such a thought stands Bible writers and Ellen White on their heads!

In fact, Ellen White could not be clearer:

> So long as Satan reigns, we shall have self to subdue, besetting sins to overcome; so long as life shall last, there will be no stopping place, no point which we can reach and say, I have fully attained. Sanctification is the result of lifelong obedience.
>
> None of the apostles and prophets ever claimed to be without sin. Men who have lived the nearest to God, men who would sacrifice life itself rather than knowingly commit a wrong act, men whom God has honored with divine light and power, have confessed the sinfulness of their nature. They have put no confidence in the flesh, have claimed no righteousness of their own, but have trusted wholly in the righteousness of Christ.
>
> So will it be with all who behold Christ. The nearer we come to Jesus, and the more clearly we discern the purity of His character, the more clearly shall we see the exceeding sinfulness of sin, and the less shall we feel like exalting ourselves. There will be a continual reaching out of the soul after God, a continual, earnest, heartbreaking confession of sin and humbling of the heart before Him. At every advance step in our Christian experience our repentance will deepen. We shall know that our sufficiency is in Christ alone and shall make the apostle's confession our own: "I know that in me (that is, in my flesh,) dwelleth no good thing." "God forbid that I should glory, save in the cross of our Lord Jesus Christ, by whom the world is crucified unto me, and I unto the world." Romans 7:18; Galatians 6:14.[7]

How does this all work? On one hand, God is working on willing Christians, building "up a strong, symmetrical character. . . . Daily [helping them to] learn the meaning of self-surrender. . . . Day by day God works . . . perfecting the character that is to stand in the time of final test. And day by day the believer is working out before men and angels a sublime experiment, showing what the gospel can do for fallen human beings."[8]

On the other hand, the maturing Christian is facing Satan's fiery darts (Ephesians 6:16), trusting completely on Jesus for his deepening repentance, knowing that without the strong arm of their heavenly

Intercessor, they surely would fail the daily test of self-surrender. Maturing Christians know that without the "all powerful Mediator,"[9] they would be "rising and falling" at best,[10] and truly miserable in their religious life—if they even remain in the church.

To say it differently, the Christian, nourished by the vine, builds branches of strength to carry the growing fruit. That is how perfect plants grow perfectly. The sun beats down, the storm weather tosses the branches, sometimes violently. But the vine and the branches and the budding fruit grow stronger, becoming ready for the heavenly Gardener.

Paul's Philippian letter, from start to finish, amplifies the biblical description of what "perfect" people are like: They keep facing the future, trusting their Lord. They keep growing. They make it a habit to let God work out His good pleasure in their lives. They never give up! They endure, regardless of earthly circumstances.

Then Paul says something very wistful, perhaps springing from what he had noticed in the early Christian church: Some did not keep pressing on; some felt that they had already attained; some put their religious experience into neutral. And they began to lose what they had.

Perhaps every reader has experienced "losing what we had." We have read many descriptions from biblical writers of what happens when we drift first into a spiritual holiday, then, soon, onto that slippery slope of unintended consequences. We can lose in an hour what had taken months, perhaps years, to gain. Not a fair trade—but such is the nature of growth.

Some plants are that way—they receive months of careful attention, but after careless neglect for a few days, they are barely recoverable. However, the good news is that no matter how much neglect we allow to settle in, God has marvelous ways to "restore to you the years that the locust hath eaten" (Joel 2:25, KJV). Our friendly Lord has not turned down one request, and won't!

We end this chapter as we began: "No finish line!" Further, God is in the business of moving His grand experiment onward in the "relentless pursuit of perfection." Two million years from now, His redeemed will be still "reaching forward to those things which are ahead" (Philippians 3:13).

And when the question is asked, "Have you ever seen a perfect person?" the only answer is, "That's God's department, not mine. All I can see is my deficiencies and the road ahead—and I know that He has not given up on me. All He asks from me is to keep abiding in Him, to continue walking with Him on the road to forever."[11]

That's the rub! This sounds almost too good to be true! Some say that they have a track record of failure—not always big-time, but enough to know that they are off the wagon as much as they are on. They know that they must have more consistency in their lives. That leads us into the next chapter. How do we develop habit patterns so that "abiding in Him" becomes second nature? And that is exactly what Jesus promised Nicodemus—a new birth, a second nature (see John 3).

---

[1] *Rediscovering Joy* (Hagerstown, Md.: Review and Herald Publishing Association, 1994), 160.

[2] *Christ's Object Lessons,* p. 307.

[3] "The germination of the seed represents the beginning of spiritual life, and the development of the plant is a beautiful figure of Christian growth. As in nature, so in grace; there can be no life without growth. The plant must either grow or die. As its growth is silent and imperceptible, but continuous, so is the development of the Christian life. At every stage of development our life may be perfect; yet if God's purpose for us is fulfilled, there will be continual advancement. Sanctification is the work of a lifetime. As our opportunities multiply, our experience will enlarge, and our knowledge increase. We shall become strong to bear responsibility, and our maturity will be in proportion to our privileges" (Ellen G. White, *Christ's Object Lessons,* pp. 65, 66).

[4] See chapter, "What Do Habits Have To Do With Assurance?"

[5] Such as Matthew 5:48; 19:21; Romans 12:2; Ephesians 4:13; Philippians 3:12, 15; Colossians 1:28; 4:12; Hebrews 2:10; 5:9; 7:19; 9:9; 10:1, 14; 11:40; 12:23; James 1:4, 17, 25; 2:22; 3:2; 1 John 4:17, 18.

[6] *Christ's Object Lessons,* p. 330.

[7] *Acts of the Apostles,* pp. 560, 561.

[8] Ibid., p. 483.

[9] Ellen G. White, *The Great Controversy,* p. 488.

[10] "Are there those here who have been sinning and repenting, sinning and repenting, and will they continue to do so till Christ shall come? May God help us that we may be truly united to Christ, the living vine, and bear fruits to the glory of God" (*Review and Herald,* April 21, 1891).

[11] For a clear presentation on the subject of Christian perfection, see J. R. Zurcher, *What Inspiration Has to Say About Christian Perfection,* translated by Edward F. White (Hagerstown, Md.: Review and Herald Publishing Association, 2002).

14

What Do Habits Have to Do With Assurance?

We have been focusing on the kind of people God makes ready to live forever. Jesus said in his famous Sermon on the Mount that people safe to save have built their lives on the rock instead of sand. Prepared people build on the rock of Christ's words, the basis of the "assurance of faith" (Hebrews 10:22).

Those who thought they were saved, living with presumptuous assurance, will discover that Jesus must say, though reluctantly: "I never knew you for what you said you were" (see Matthew 7:23). Their lives were based on principles that were primarily self-centered. They did their good works to impress others, either their friends or God Himself. Their lives amounted only to sand castles to be washed away by the restless sea.

Those who built on principles and truth that were rock-secured, not only endured the troubles of this life—they are safe to save.[1] In practical terms, what was the difference in the lives of those with presumptuous assurance (sand castles) and those with genuine assurance (rock-assurance)? What was going on in their neural patterns that made them think and act the way they did?

Let's first ask a question that we have looked at before. What does it mean to build on the rock?

Building on the rock is the same as "abiding in Christ."[2] Ellen White is very insightful regarding how we are to build on the rock (after discussing Christ's analogy of rock and sand):

We build on Christ by obeying His word. It is not he who merely enjoys righteousness, that is righteous, but he who does righteousness. Holiness is not rapture; it is the result of surrendering all to God; it is doing the will of our heavenly Father.

Religion consists in doing the words of Christ; not doing to earn God's favor, but because, all undeserving, we have received the gift of His love. Christ places the salvation of man, not upon profession merely, but upon faith that is made manifest in works of righteousness. Doing, not saying merely, is expected of the followers of Christ. It is through action that character is built. . . . As you receive the word in faith, it will give you power to obey. As you give heed to the light you have, greater light will come. You are building on God's word, and your character will be builded after the similitude of the character of Christ.[3]

It would be hard to misunderstand these two paragraphs! Our question is: How is this done? How does it happen—in my life and yours—that "through action . . . character is built"?

That is a powerful concept. Not through words only, not even through Bible study and prayer only—but through "action . . . character is built"! How do actions affect character?

The word is "habit." Those who are eventually redeemed will be habitually "keep[ing] the commandments of God and the faith of Jesus" (Revelation 14:12, present tense, "making a life-habit of keeping"). So let's talk about habits!

Habits cannot be measured like muscles or observed on a electrocardiogram. *Habit* is a word that describes what happens when thoughts or acts are repeated. Habits are truly good friends! Think of the time we save (without taking time to think about our actions as we once did) when we tie our shoes, drive cars, use the typewriter or computer, etc.! Remember the hours and weeks it took to develop these skills that we no longer have to *consciously* repeat, over and over, just to get it right! I like the way Ellen White put it:

> The power of self-restraint strengthens by exercise. That which at first seems difficult, by constant repetition grows easy and right thoughts and actions become habitual.[4]

Habits are our built-in, antistress kits. To the extent wholesome habits control our lives, to that extent we enjoy life. I don't mean that we can be happy all the time, but we can live with a deep sense of joy about the bigger issues of life—all the time! If we are not enjoying life, we may be plugged into the wrong socket. Some other power may be giving us energy!

Habits have lasting consequences: "Actions repeated form habits, habits form character, and by the character our destiny for time and for eternity is decided."[5]

When we remember that God will not and cannot save rebels, the issue of "character" becomes profoundly important—especially when we remember that when Jesus comes "He is not to cleanse us of our sins, to remove from us the defects in our characters, or to cure us of the infirmities of our tempers and dispositions."[6]

How are habits made or unmade? Wise Solomon said that as a man thinks, "so is he" (Proverbs 23:7). We think with brain cells that lie about an inch behind our forehead. These brain cells are the capital of the body, the power center for all that happens to every nerve and muscle. The brain's messages are sent "electrically" at astonishing speeds that scientists have not yet been able to replicate on the most advanced computer. And we have some computers making billions of decisions every second!

Most of the illnesses that physicians see in their offices are mentally or emotionally induced (psychosomatic). We have all experienced the truth of this fact. When our willpower is at low ebb; when the mind or emotions wrestle with bad news, we have difficulty resisting cold symptoms, or an upset stomach. But this same principle can reverse physical problems. With habits of positive attitudes and trust in God, our bodies respond to our thoughts, and we resist disease and overcome illnesses.[7]

So how does the brain do this work? The entire brain operates on ten watts of electricity and performs math calculations that far outrun the world's largest computers. Each brain cell has many fibers called dendrites which constantly receive all kinds of information. One long fiber called the axon transmits messages between cells.[8]

The microscope shows us that on the end of the axon are tiny enlargements called boutons (French, for "buttons"). These boutons secrete chemicals (ACH and GABA) which stimulate the next cell to send a message down the nerve path to whatever muscle or organ is to be activated. But there is no direct connection between the axon and the next cell's dendrites, only a tiny space, called the synapse. How does the message get across this synapse? Through the chemicals of the boutons.

Here is where it gets interesting. Some axons have more boutons than others. Why? Because that axon has been stimulated more than others. More stimulation, more boutons. With more boutons, the easier it is the next time for similar messages to flow along that particular pathway. Habits are forming!

How are boutons formed? Any thought or act forms a bouton. Thoughts and acts often repeated build more boutons on the end of that particular axon so that it becomes easier to repeat that same thought or act when the same situation is again faced. Just like cutting across the lawn eventually wears a worn path, so repeated thoughts actually produce physical and chemical changes in our nerve pathways. Thoughts don't vanish into thin air, they are etched into a biochemical pattern that we call habits.

The good news and the bad news is that boutons never disappear. Right! Frightening, as well as assuring! For example, recovered alcoholics tell each other that they "are always" alcoholics. So they avoid friends who drink and places where alcohol is likely to be served. Chocoholics and those involved in "fatal attractions" never lose those boutons that make it easier for them to "cave in."[9]

But the good news is that the bad-habit boutons can be overpowered by good-habit boutons. Those who find it easy to be angry, to be lazy or self-centered, can believe that with the right set of the mind and the power of God, new habits of self-control, industriousness, and caring can be established firmly. *We are what we think.*

Sounds too easy? Here is how we build more yes or no boutons, whichever is appropriate for the occasion. For example, when we are used to saying "Yes" to bad choices, we must build "No" boutons.

Research indicates that we can change most any habit in a matter of weeks—some say twenty-one days![10] When we choose to resist temptation (that is, whatever obscures "abiding in Christ"), when we say, "No!" the GABA secretion is secreted at the synapse. GABA puts the brakes on and keeps that cell from firing. With repeated resistance (repeated "No's" when before, the choices were "Yes's"), more "No" boutons are formed. With more "No" boutons on the end of that axon that had formerly led to inappropriate sexual behavior or quick anger, GABA (the brakes) is even more powerful, making it virtually impossible to do wrong in that particular situation again.

Sound too simple? There is a warning. The GABA secretion does not function well, most often not at all, when we lose sleep or get fatigued for whatever reason, good or bad. GABA (the brake on our decision making) is affected by fatigue much sooner than ACH (the accelerator on our decision making). That is, when we are tired, we find it easier to do and say what we please, long after we have lost our braking power. That is why committee meetings in the evenings, Saturday night flings, and nighttime confrontations with others (children, spouses, etc.) most often turn into regrettable experiences. When we are tired, the go-for-it, tell-it-like-it-is, have-fun attitude has no GABA to say No!

To get even more practical, most of life is a matter of conflicting choices—shall I, or shall I not? One brain cell says, "Why not? Go for it!" The other says, "No, you'd better not!" Which one wins? The one with the most boutons built up by habit! One brain cell sees the extra piece of scrumptious pecan pie or the banana sundae; or the possibility of getting a better grade by cheating because everyone is doing it; or eating between meals and skipping breakfast; or undue familiarity with the opposite sex, etc. However, another brain cell now becomes activated; it sees the same opportunities and says, "No, there's a better way. I choose to abide in Christ and all those negative choices will keep me from my full potential. I want to honor my parents (or my spouse, or my God). I want to be trusted."

All this choosing (mental activity) takes electrical energy. When negative temptation of any kind says, "Go for it! Looks good; take a piece!" or, "Go for it, no one will ever know," thirty millivolts, shall we say, of ACH energy surges into your action cell. But your better self says (if you are not in fatigue), "Hold it, there are consequences down the road I don't want to live with. Don't fire! [that is, "Don't cheat," "Don't take that extra piece, etc."]." If the better brain cell has more boutons, GABA jumps into action with forty millivolts, shall we say, of electrical power, saying, "No!" Because it takes only ten millivolts for a cell to fire, the brain cell with the most boutons wins![11]

The scenario, of course, can be reversed. If the brain cell saying, "Go for it!" has the most boutons, ACH wins. Especially if the brain cells are tired and GABA is not functioning.

Let's consider this again! All it takes to say "No" *when you should* is a difference of ten millivolts of electrical power. The brain cell is making a fast algebraic decision in a matter of a thousandth of a second— and the ten millivolts will win.

This is how habits are formed. More boutons (because of the same thoughts and actions repeated often) equal more electric current to say "No" or "Yes" at the proper times. The more boutons producing a certain habit pattern, the more spontaneous, habitual, and natural will be the ability to make right decisions in the future. That is how right decisions form right habits that form right characters.[12]

The eminent Harvard psychologist, William James, observed:

> Could the young but realize how soon they will become mere
> walking bundles of habits, they would give more heed to their
> conduct while in the plastic state. We are spinning our fates,
> good or evil, and never to be undone. Every smallest stroke of
> virtue or vice leaves its never-so-little scar. . . . The drunken Rip
> Van Winkel, in Jefferson's play, excuses himself for every fresh
> dereliction by saying, "I won't count this time!" Well! He may
> not count it, and a kind Heaven may not count it; but it is being
> counted nonetheless. Down among his nerve cells and fibers
> the molecules are counting it, registering and storing it up to
> be used against him when the next temptation comes. Nothing
> we ever do, in strict scientific literalness is wiped out.
>
> Of course, this has its good sides as well as its bad one. As we
> become permanent drunkards by so many separate drinks, so
> we become saints in the moral, and authorities and experts in
> the practical and scientific spheres, by so many separate acts
> and hours of work.[13]

However, Christians should be realists—negative habits are always
there in the shadows, because all boutons remain in place.[14] We may
repent and set our feet in right paths but the familiarity with the former
temptations is a crease in the paper that cannot be completely unfolded.[15] That is why wise Paul could say, "Let him who thinks he stands
take heed lest he fall" (1 Corinthians 10:12).

At this point, at this crucial knife edge of each person's future on
which all else balances, we must be very clear and honest with ourselves: Willpower, no matter how strong a person is, will never be sufficient to build enough boutons so that we will be above temptation. We
live in a very dynamic universe, and forces beyond the human are im-
pressing us constantly (Ephesians 6:12, 13).

Only by the empowering of the personal intervention of the
Holy Spirit, the Eternal Energy of the universe, can any of us be
prompted even to begin wanting to make the right boutons along
the right axons. Even God chooses not to make the right boutons
for us—if we do not *choose* His way. This choosing, this response to
the prompting of the Spirit, is the first step in making new boutons.
*God does not choose for us any more than He does our breathing for
us!*[16]

The good news is that He has wired us to succeed with a neural
system that defies human imagination or duplication. All He wants

from us is our choice. Each right choice becomes another bouton, until the "weight" of boutons forms a strong and good habit.

Our brain cells make all this happen. You would think that caring for our brain cells would be our highest priority. How can we make healthy brain cells every day? First, make sure that we are feeding them with rich, pure blood. How do we do that? By eating food that is healthful, such as fruit, nuts, vegetables, and grains. By avoiding animal products that send cholesterol and other undesirable elements zinging through our blood stream. By drinking plenty of water daily. By breathing deeply in fresh air. By exercising daily so that all that water, good nutrients, and fresh oxygen is hurried through the blood stream, feeding those brain cells minute by minute!

When brain cells are not fed properly, we doze at the wheel of our car, in class lectures, or in church; we make poor decisions; we become lazy, grouchy, and miserable.

But brain cells are even more important than helping us to think clearly and quickly. They are not only where habits are formed. *Brain cells must be kept healthy because the brain is the only place in our bodies where the Holy Spirit connects with us.*

Let the following quotation sink in:

> The brain nerves that connect with the whole system are the medium through which heaven communicates with man and affects the inmost life. Whatever hinders the circulation of the electric current in the nervous system, thus weakening the vital powers and lessening mental susceptibility, makes it more difficult to arouse the moral nature.[17]

Think about it! Anything we do to improve our general health makes it easier to hear the Holy Spirit! When I discovered that principle some years ago, I surely paid more attention to what I ate, how I exercised, and when I rested. The thought also occurred to me that when I violated simple health rules, I was tuning down the Holy Spirit and thus not getting the confirming voice of assurance that I want to live with day by day (see 1 John 3:24).

Imagine that! How I treat my physical body directly affects my mental and moral sensibilities and thus my character development. And without question, my daily sense of a saving relationship with Jesus. That sounds very much like "doing" the will of God (see Philippians 2:13) and building on the rock that Jesus talked about (see Matthew 7:21, 24).

Through it all, God holds before us, day and night, the reasons why we should choose His way of making sense out of our lives. He never wearies. He is always ready to provide the electrical energy that jump-starts our electrical system whenever we choose to plug into His power. And He never gives up on us, even if we fail again and again in the self-correcting process of reaching our goals. He is already there to jump-start us again with more energy to make more boutons of the right kind. That is what Paul meant when he said, "God is at work in you, both to will and to do His good pleasure."[18]

The good news is that the more we get into the practice of permitting the Lord to help us say "Yes" to His plans for us, the easier it becomes to keep adding boutons on the right axons. That is why we must make a daily habit of focusing on those things that are true, honest, just, pure, lovely, and of a good report, as Paul put it so eloquently (see Philippians 4:8). Each act of focusing becomes a new bouton until what one focuses on becomes a fixed habit and is reflected in the Christian's character.

One added thought. Some very nice people still honestly believe that it is impossible for sinful, human beings to overcome sinful attitudes, actions, feelings, etc. Contrary to the golden thread throughout the Bible that "overcomers" will occupy the new earth,[19] they hope that in some way all their sinful habits for which they keep asking forgiveness will be erased from their frontal lobes in the resurrection. This is perilously close to thinking like the presumptuous "believers" who want to know why the Lord does not "know" them (Matthew 7:22).

The gold standard, the rock of truth, is that the Holy Spirit's awesome task is to redirect our neural patterns so that it becomes a habit to think righteously (right-wisely). Whether we want to believe it or not, the day is coming when those prepared for the Lord to come will have settled "into the truth, both intellectually and spiritually, so they cannot be moved."[20] Or, more settled into self-centered, envious, hateful persons, so they, too, cannot be moved!

How does this happen in my life and in yours? By the development of a habit pattern in thinking and doing that will never change.[21] In many ways, Ellen White is consistent and clear:

> If our hearts are softened and subdued by the grace of Christ, and glowing with a sense of God's goodness and love, there will be a *natural* outflow of love, sympathy, and tenderness to others.[22]

The grace of Christ must mold the entire being, and its triumph will not be complete until the heavenly universe shall witness *habitual* tenderness of feeling, Christlike love, and holy deeds in the deportment of the children of God.[23]

That which at first seems difficult, by constant repetition grows easy, until right thoughts and actions become *habitual.* If we will we may turn away from all that is cheap and inferior, and rise to a high standard; we may be respected by men and beloved of God.[24]

When self is merged in Christ, love springs forth *spontaneously.* The completeness of Christian character is attained when the impulse to help and bless others *springs constantly* from within—when the sunshine of heaven fills the heart and is revealed in the countenance.[25]

The principles of God's law will dwell in the heart, and control the actions. It will then be as *natural* for us to seek purity and holiness, to shun the spirit and example of the world, and to seek to benefit all around us, as it is for the angels of glory to execute the mission of love assigned them. None will enter the city of God but those who have been doers of the word.[26]

This is powerful good news! We don't have to be grouchy, stingy, self-centered, or angry forever. Not when the Holy Spirit gets to work!

I know that some readers have some anxious thoughts regarding how all this fits into some scary feelings regarding the investigative judgment. They think: How can anybody have solid assurance today when nothing is settled until our names "come up" in the pre-Advent judgment? I don't want anyone to worry about the investigative judgment. So let's take a look at this subject in our next chapter.

---

[1] See pp. 51, 68.
[2] See pp. 23, 47–50.
[3] *Thoughts From the Mount of Blessing,* pp. 149, 150.
[4] *The Ministry of Healing,* p. 491,
[5] Ellen G. White, *Christ's Object Lessons,* p. 356.
[6] Ellen G. White, *Testimonies for the Church,* vol. 2, p. 355; see also p. 83.

[7] "Right and correct habits, intelligently and perseveringly practiced, will be removing the cause of disease and the strong drugs will not be resorted to" (Ellen G. White, *Medical Ministry*, p. 222; see also *Testimonies*, vol. 3, p. 157).

[8] "The brain is the capital of the body, the seat of all the nervous forces and of mental action. The nerves proceeding from the brain control the body. By the brain nerves, mental impressions are conveyed to all the nerves of the body as by telegraph wires; and they control the vital action of every part of the system. All the organs of motion are governed by the communications they receive from the brain" (Ellen G. White, *Testimonies*, vol. 3, p. 69; see also *Education*, p. 197).

[9] "Let none flatter themselves that sins cherished for a time can easily be given up by and by. This is not so. Every sin cherished weakens the character and strengthens habit; and physical, mental, and moral depravity is the result. You may repent of the wrong you have done, and set your feet in right paths; but the mold of your mind and your familiarity with evil will make it difficult for you to distinguish between right and wrong. Through the wrong habits formed, Satan will assail you again and again" (Ellen G. White, *Christ's Object Lessons*, p. 281).

[10] While preparing this page I read an article on "permanent weight loss." It reported that researchers have found that it takes about twelve weeks to break even lifelong dietary habits.

[11] Elden M. Chalmers and Esther L. Chalmers, *Making the Most of Family Living* (Nampa, Idaho: Pacific Press Publishing Association, 1979), pp. 61–67.

[12] "The power of self-restraint strengthens by exercise. That which at first seems difficult, by constant repetition grows easy, until right thoughts and actions become habitual. If we will we may turn away from all that is cheap and inferior, and rise to a high standard; we may be respected by men and beloved of God" (*The Ministry of Healing*, p. 491).

[13] Chalmers, pp. 66, 67.

[14] "We should not be slow in breaking up a sinful habit. Unless evil habits are conquered, they will conquer us, and destroy our happiness" (Ellen G. White, *Testimonies*, vol. 4, p. 654).

[15] "What the child sees and hears is drawing deep lines upon the tender mind, which no after circumstances in life can entirely efface. The intellect is now taking shape, and the affections receiving direction and strength. Repeated acts in a given course become habits. These may be modified by severe training, in afterlife, but are seldom changed" (Ellen G. White, *Child Guidance*, pp. 199, 200).

[16] "While these youth [four Hebrew youth in Babylon] were working out their own salvation, God was working in them to will and to do of His good pleasure. Here are revealed the conditions of success. To make God's grace our own, we must act our part. The Lord does not propose to perform for us either the willing or the doing. His grace is given to work in us to will and to do, but never as a substitute for our effort. Our souls are to be aroused to cooperate. The Holy Spirit works in us, that we may work out our own salvation. This is the practical lesson the Holy Spirit is striving to teach us" (Ellen G. White Comments, *SDA Bible Commentary*, vol. 4, p. 1167).

[17] Ellen G. White, *Education*, p. 209.

[18] Philippians 2:13.

[19] See Revelation 2:7, 11, 17, 26; 3:5, 12, 21.

[20] Ellen G. White, *The Faith I Live By*, p. 287. In fact, God is waiting for such people who will permit the Holy Spirit to complete His work in them (Philippians 1:6). See *Christ's Object Lessons*, p. 69.

[21] Of course, this equally applies to maturing wheat as well as to maturing tares, to those becoming more like Jesus or those becoming more like Satan.

[22] *Testimonies,* vol. 5, p. 606 (italics supplied).

[23] *God's Amazing Grace,* p. 235 (italics supplied).

[24] *The Ministry of Healing,* p. 491 (italics supplied).

[25] *Christ's Object Lessons,* p. 384 (italics supplied).

[26] *Review and Herald,* October 23, 1888 (italics supplied).

CHAPTER FIFTEEN

Investigative Judgment– Good News!

I remember the afternoon well. The sun was streaming through my office window at Pacific Union College. I was busily correcting examination papers when the door burst open. A former theological student, now graduated, flung himself into the chair beside my desk. I had not seen him for several years. His face was wrinkled with despair. Out poured his anguish. He had been in jail for a few months. Over and over he repeated that probation had closed for him! He was certain now that his name had "come up" in the investigative judgment and that he was a lost man!

He was always a very likable young man—full of courtesies and smiles. But somehow, after graduation, an intense battle had been fought over his soul. In reflecting on all this, his new agony was caused by a wrong understanding of what Jesus had been wanting to do for him as his High Priest in the heavenly sanctuary. This led to a scary understanding of the pre-Advent, investigative judgment.

What notion had muddled his thinking? Unfortunately, the thinking is not unique to him, and it goes like this: Since 1844, angels have been turning pages in the books of heaven, each page representing the record of each person's life, beginning with Adam and Eve. Pages turning, day and night! Each person's future—eternal life or damnation—is settled after each page is examined. Never tiring, the angels move through the years until the present. When the pages of the living come up, it's judgment time—ready or not! In some way, the whole universe looks at all our sins. If one is judged to be unfit for eternal life on the day one's name "comes up," probation is over. The

Holy Spirit no longer speaks to that person—his probation is closed. The unsaved now live out their desires and passions, unrestrained by the Holy Spirit speaking to the conscience. So the scary notion goes.

I think I have heard the echo of my young friend's agony in certain sermons through the years. Perhaps a camp meeting sermon: "Get right with God today, at this camp meeting! Who knows when your name will come up in the judgment? It may be tonight! You may never have another camp meeting!"

What is wrong here? It is hard to know where to begin! Let me list some obvious misunderstandings, most of which we have already discussed in this book:

- God doesn't close our probation—we do. Grace will keep pressing its appeal, night and day, never holding back its promises of pardon and power—unless men and women tune out the Spirit's pleading. God's gracious promises are always on the table, His front door is always open, His light is always on: " 'The one who comes to Me I will by no means cast out' " (John 6:37).[1] To be perfectly clear, men and women who are making a habit of saying "No" to the Spirit, who stubbornly resist whatever light of truth they have, *are closing their own probation. Not God!*
- Therefore, as far as the living are concerned, the investigative judgment is not focused on angels, or even God, turning pages but on the maturing of a person's life. The one question is: Is that person maturing into one who can be trusted with eternal life?[2]
- God the Father is not the judge " 'for the Father judges no one, but has committed all judgment to the Son' " (John 5:22, 27-30). But the kind of "judgment" given to Jesus is not like an earthly court (as we shall see). " 'For God did not send His Son into the world to condemn the world, but that the world through Him might be saved' " (John 3:17).
- If Jesus is not the frowning judge so often seen in medieval art,[3] how then, does He do His job of saving the world (which is His way of "judging" the world)? By bringing light "to every man coming into the world" (John 1:9), by revealing truth in some way to everyone on which moral decisions are made. Thus, *those who reject this light are condemning (judging) themselves* (see John 3:18-21).
- Contrary to some allegations of the past few years, Christ's record does not stand in place of our records when our names come up in the investigative judgment.[4] Truly, as we have seen in earlier chapters, we are not to be saved by our works, but we surely will be judged by our works: "They were judged each one according

to his works" (Revelation 20:13). "For we must all appear before the judgment seat of Christ, that each one may receive the things done in the body, according to what he has done, whether good or bad" (2 Corinthians 5:10). " 'For the Son of man will come in the glory of His Father with His angels; and then He will reward each according to his works' " (Matthew 16:27). The redeemed will be more than admirers of Jesus; they will be His followers who are determined to overcome evil even as He has overcome (see Revelation 3:21).

The whole point of the gospel is to restore men and women to the place where they can be trusted to say "Yes" to God's will as forever examples of divine-human cooperation.[5]

This does not mean that we "deserve" salvation or that we have in any way "earned" eternal life. Hardly! The righteousness of Christ alone provides our "title" to heaven and our "fitness" for heaven is made possible by His grace that supplies the power to overcome; otherwise, each of the redeemed would stand naked before the scrutiny of the universe. The investigative judgment separates those who have claimed the Lord's name but not His character (see Matthew 7:21-23) from those who have seriously and genuinely accepted the way of the Cross, and like Paul, "die daily" (1 Corinthians 15:31) to all self-centered, self-glorifying desires. The issue is not who has absolute perfection but who has, with the time lived, given the angels, the unfallen worlds, and God Himself, a trajectory of what his or her life would be if time were to be continued. This kind of genuine faith describes the thief on the cross as well as Enoch. That spread of experience will include every one of us!

In contrast to these misunderstandings, here are some basic thoughts that we must understand before we get too far into our description of what has been going on in heaven since 1844:

* The judgment books (see Revelation 20:12) record our choices, whether we are becoming more like Jesus or more like His adversary, the devil. The Bible uses various analogies, such as sheep and goats (Matthew 25:32, 33), wheat and tares (Matthew 13:24-30), and the seal of God and the mark of the beast (Revelation 7:3; 13:16, 17; 14:9). How these records are kept are beyond our imagination. However, with modern computer memory systems, with trillions of computations performed virtually simultaneously, we get a faint idea of how the mind of God "records" the DNA plus character configuration of everyone who has ever lived. Then when

we think of the marvels of modern CD or video recordings and storage, we get further glimpses of how any episode since Creation can be replayed instantly. Nothing will be subject to guesswork. As Jesus said, " 'For by your words you will be justified, and by your words you will be condemned' " (Matthew 12:37).[6]

- Jesus does not arbitrarily balance out one's good deeds and bad deeds in determining one's eternal future. One's future is determined by whether a person's character is becoming safe to save or not, whether his or her life trajectory shows a person who, if time were given, could be trusted with eternal life.[7] "The character is revealed, not by occasional good deeds and occasional misdeeds, but by the tendency of the habitual words and acts."[8]

When those who claim to be children of God become Christlike in character, they will be obedient to God's commandments. Then the Lord can trust them to be of the number who shall compose the family of heaven. . . . They have a right to join the blood-washed throng. . . . He expects us to overcome in His name. Those who reject the gift of Christ's righteousness are rejecting the attributes of character which would constitute them the sons and daughters of God. They are rejecting that which alone could give them a fitness for a place at the marriage feast. . . . There will be no future probation in which to prepare for eternity. It is in this life that we are to put on the robe of Christ's righteousness. This is our only opportunity to form characters for the home which Christ has made ready for those who obey His commandments.[9]

- Adventists do believe that sins are forgiven when they are confessed and forsaken. Adventists don't wait until the investigative judgment to know with certainty that their sins are covered by the mercies of Jesus. Further, they rejoice with New Testament writers who describe Christ's atoning (or, reconciling) work as twofold: not only for Christ's forgiveness but also for His cleansing (Proverbs 28:13; 1 John 1:9). *Cleansing* is John's word for "grace to help in time of need" (Hebrews 4:16).
- Jesus has done this wonderful ministry of forgiveness and cleansing (empowering) since He ascended to heaven. But since 1844, He has added a new phase to His work as our Mediator. In addition to His two-fold ministry since the Cross, the investigative judgment is now concerned with the judgment of character and the preparation of a people to meet Him at the Second Advent.

It is absolutely essential that we understand why Satan is doing his fiercest to muddle our thinking regarding the investigative judgment. The college graduate I mentioned at the beginning of this chapter is a classic example of what happens when wrong notions are believed. How does Satan go about this nefarious work?

- He "invents unnumbered schemes to occupy our minds that they may not dwell upon the very work with which we ought to be best acquainted."[10] Can you think of dozens of peripheral topics that we so easily would rather discuss than what Jesus is doing now in the heavenly sanctuary?
- He "hates the great truths that bring to view an atoning sacrifice and an all-powerful Mediator."[11] Can you see the importance of the ellipse of truth wherein two great truths must be kept in equal focus?
- He will divert our minds from the fact that "the subject of the sanctuary and the investigative judgment should be clearly understood by the people of God."[12]
- Why is he doing his utmost to fog our minds regarding the investigative judgment? Because he knows that if he succeeds, "it will be impossible for [us] to exercise the faith which is essential at this time, or to occupy the position which God designs [us] to fill."[13]
- He doesn't mind if we sing songs about the Cross and focus on Jesus as our Savior, as long as we don't join His work as "atoning sacrifice" with His role as our "all-powerful Mediator." Why? Because he knows that gazing at Jesus on His cross ("atoning sacrifice") without following Him to heaven as our High Priest ("all-powerful Mediator") will divert us from understanding the power of the gospel and the primary work of the Holy Spirit. Satan will do anything and everything to keep us from recognizing that "the intercession of Christ in man's behalf in the sanctuary above is as essential to the plan of salvation as was His death upon the Cross. By His death He began that work which after His resurrection he ascended to complete in heaven."[14]
- *Let that thought sink in. Keep your eyes on where Jesus now is and what He is now doing on our behalf!*

Before we go further, it is essential that we understand why other biblical scholars have *rejected* the concept of the investigative judgment. The late Donald Grey Barnhouse, former editor of *Eternity* magazine, described this doctrine as "the most colossal, psychological, face-saving phenomenon in religious history."[15] In this book we have already reflected on certain presuppositions of Barnhouse and others that have kept them from seeing the biblical need for the investigative judgment. Their problem is threefold:

- True, the Scriptures do not mention the term, "the investigative judgment," but the need for the pre-Advent judgment is called for throughout the Bible. In addition to various biblical texts we have already noted, consider Christ's words to the Sadducees calling for an investigative judgment prior to the end-time events regarding those who are " 'counted worthy to . . . the resurrection from the dead' " (Luke 20:35; see also Luke 21:36; Acts 5:41). When are people "counted worthy" prior to the resurrection?

- Because Barnhouse and others believe that Christ made a final atonement on the cross, they seem to be blinded to our Lord's ministry in the heavenly sanctuary as set forth in the book of Hebrews. As we have seen already, and will see later, the work of Christ in the heavenly sanctuary is as essential as His work on the cross.[16] Limited gospels lead to incomplete pictures of what Jesus is doing now.

- The investigative judgment concept is built into the core Adventist belief that before Jesus returns a worldwide movement will reflect the messages of the three angels in Revelation 14. Those messages, as well as the rest of the Bible, emphasize how important God's loyal followers are to Him as well as to the world as they proclaim God's last-day appeal before the crash and horror of the seven last plagues. God will have a prepared people. The investigative judgment reflects this preparation on earth and the whole unfallen universe endorses God's judgments regarding their fitness to live forever.

So what really has been happening since 1844? Many good books have been written on the significance of 1844 as the terminal date for the majestic time prophecy of Daniel 8:14.[17] Our concern here is to focus on what has been going on in heaven since 1844.

- *From the standpoint of angels,* some kind of investigative judgment must occur before Jesus comes. How else would the angels know which people since Adam to resurrect in the first resurrection?[18]

- *From the standpoint of people on earth,* some kind of examination should be going on in their lives. If ever we take Paul's advice it should be now: "Examine yourselves as to whether you are in the faith. Prove yourselves" (2 Corinthians 13:5). And Peter's counsel: "Therefore brethren, be even more diligent to make your calling and election sure, for if you do these things you will never stumble" (2 Peter 1:10). And Ellen White's encouragement: "Through the grace of God and their own diligent effort they must be conquerors in the battle with evil. While the investigative judgment is going forward in heaven . . . there is to be a special work of purification, of putting away of sin, among God's people upon earth. . . . When this work shall have been accomplished, the followers of Christ will be ready for His appearing."[19]

- *From the standpoint of God in heaven,* another kind of investigative judgment must occur before Jesus comes. The first angel of Revelation 14 announced that " 'the hour of *His judgment* has come' " (verse 7, italics supplied).

What could the angel mean? Yes, the time would come, prior to the Advent, when God permits Himself to be placed on trial! Can we imagine greater love or humility than this—that the Creator of the universe should put Himself in the dock and have all the universe judge whether He has been fair, just, and merciful in His dealings with sinners?

John tells us how this "trial" turns out. The judgment of the universe is: " 'Great and marvelous are Your works, Lord God Almighty! Just and true are Your ways, O King of the saints' " (Revelation 15:3); " 'Alleluia! Salvation and glory and honor and power belong to the Lord our God! For true and righteous are His judgments' " (Revelation 19:1, 2). But what kind of trial did God go through before He was accorded this magnificent acquittal?

We must keep our eyes on the big picture. Whatever else we may learn about the pre-Advent, investigative judgment, the primary focus is on how this remarkable event vindicates God's side of His controversy with Satan. This is done with a double emphasis:

- The eyes of the universe are on God's judgment as to whom He says are safe to save. Our Lord's evidence will be endorsed by onlooking angels and beings on other inhabited worlds;
- The eyes of the universe will see the consequences of rebellion in final display, ending with the din and crash of the seven last plagues. Satan's argument from the beginning has been that God intimidates, that He asks for the impossible from created beings, and thus He is unfair in the way He runs the universe. And now it is showdown time![20]

C. S. Lewis noted that "ancient man approached God (or even the gods) as the accused person approaches his judge. For the modern man the roles are reversed. He is the judge: God is in the dock. . . . Man is on the Bench and God in the Dock."[21] If Lewis could have seen the bigger picture, he would see how his insights would have taken on universal proportions. In a very real sense, during the investigative judgment, God indeed is in the dock, as we shall now see.

This emphasis on the big picture—final vindication of God's justice, patience, and loving wisdom—is foretold in Daniel and Ezekiel, and amplified in Revelation.

In Daniel 7:9-27, we trace the prophet's grand vision of the court session in heaven prior to the end of the last days. This overview of a court session wherein the Son of man, symbolically depicted, enters a new phase of our Lord's mediatorial work is not describing Christ's second advent.[22] (No reference is made to the symbolic "stone" of Daniel 2:44, 45 or to any other indication that Daniel is referring to the first resurrection or to the end of this world as we now know it.) This court scene is describing the events begun on October 22, 1844.[23]

The investigative judgment is not necessary to inform an all-wise God who are eligible to live forever. He certainly knows what has been written in "the books." But He wants every angel and every inhabitant of unfallen worlds to see the evidence, to make up their own mind as to whether Jesus is fair when He makes up His kingdom.

Whose names are in " 'the books [that] were opened' " (Daniel 7:10) leading to the " 'judgment . . . made in favor of the saints' " (Daniel 7:22)? These books called the book of life (Revelation 20:12) contain the names of "all those who have ever entered the service of God.[24] (The names of sinners who have never responded to God's entreaties, who have never asked for His pardon and power, are not recorded in the book of life.)

Again, "the books" are opened in the pre-Advent judgment for two special reasons:

- to give angels and created beings in unfallen worlds an opportunity to review God's judgments "made in favor of the saints of the Most High" (after all, they are really interested in who their eternal neighbors will be);
- to prepare the angels for those who will be raised in the first resurrection (Matthew 24:31).

Throughout the Bible God has made it clear that He is interested in character, not mere words or even acts that are only a pretense of full commitment. On different occasions, Jesus spoke of those who professed loyalty but who did not practice their profession. He likened them to the foolish who built on sand (Matthew 7:26), to tares who at first looked like wheat but more fully revealed in the harvest (Matthew 13:30), to the five foolish bridesmaids (Matthew 25:10), to the lazy servant entrusted with talent (Matthew 25:30), and to "goats" (Matthew 25:46).

All these representations of those who had once professed loyalty to God had their names in "the books" (probably considered "members in good and regular standing" in their local churches!), but their characters did not reflect what they "believed."[25] During the investigative judgment, their life records are reviewed and found wanting. Their names are " '[blotted] out . . . from the Book of Life' " (Revelation 3:5).[26]

Daniel wrote about other matters that will be accomplished during the time of the investigative judgment. In some magnificent way, the universe will be cleansed from all the lies and misrepresentations that Satan has heaped upon God, on one hand, and on God's people, on the other. His final witness to the power of the gospel (Matthew 24:14; Romans 1:16) will be manifested through those whose neural patterns are cleansed of desires and habits that once were in contradiction to God's will.[27]

The word used for "cleansed" in Daniel 8:14 has "such a breadth of meaning that it cannot be captured by a single English word." The Hebrew, *nitsdaq,* conveys at least three English "nuances" such as "(1) to 'set right/restore' (as emphasized in Isa. 46:13), (2) to 'cleanse' (as emphasized in Job 15:14; 4:17; and 17:9), and (3) to 'vindicate' (as in Isa. 50:8)."[28]

In view of the great controversy, all three "nuances" together convey exactly what transpires during Christ's role as our High Priest during the investigative judgment.

- "To set right or to be restored."[29] Since 1844, the first angel of Revelation 14 proclaims that once again the world will hear the full-orbed, "everlasting gospel." For centuries this world has heard a limited gospel, one that focuses primarily on forgiveness while muting the empowering grace that God has promised to overcomers.[30] But the "everlasting gospel" truly "restores" the truth about God's salvation plan—more than "cheap grace,"[31] more than rigorous pilgrimages, more than good fellowship and warm spiritual feelings, etc.
- "To cleanse."[32] In this text, so much of the Old Testament typology looms, depicting how the "sins" of the people, transferred to the sanctuary

during the year, are finally "cleansed" on the annual Day of Atonement.[33] When we look at the larger picture that God intended the sanctuary service to teach us, we learn that "the tabernacle, through its service of sacrifice, was to teach—the lesson of pardon of sin, and power through the Saviour for obedience unto life"[34]

The earthly sanctuary revealed many aspects of Christ's role as our Sacrifice and Mediator for one transcending purpose: "In all [earthly sanctuary services], God desired His people to read His purpose for the human soul."[35] It was the same purpose that Paul emphasized when he wrote, "Do you not know that you are the temple of God and that the Spirit of God dwells in you?" (1 Corinthians 3:16).

Ellen White connects the earthly sanctuary with its divine purpose even more directly when she notes that the "Jewish tabernacle was a type of the Christian church," that those "faithful and loyal to God" form the " 'true tabernacle,' " and "Christ is the . . . high priest of all who believe in Him as a personal Saviour."[36]

During the pre-Advent judgment, unfallen worlds and the angels are reviewing (investigating) our maturing characters to see if we truly are serious about joining them in a sin-free universe.

Especially will this be true of those whom Christ is preparing to represent Him during the end time when His witnesses will indeed proclaim the "everlasting gospel" to all the world (Matthew 24:14). In fact, the successful completion of the gospel commission depends on "cleansed" Christians who want God's character as well as His power. Only then will their witnessing be believable.[37]

In a special sense, in view of the larger, antitypical meaning of the sanctuary symbolism, the investigative judgment since 1844 is a matter of "cleansing" the human temple from the defilement of sin.

In a sermon delivered at the Minneapolis General Conference in 1888, Ellen White emphasized this point:

> Now Christ is in the heavenly sanctuary. And what is He doing? Making atonement for us, cleansing the sanctuary from the sins of the people. Then we must enter by faith into the sanctuary with Him, we must commence the work in the sanctuary of our souls. We are to cleanse ourselves from all defilement. We must "cleanse ourselves from all filthiness of the flesh and spirit, perfecting holiness in the fear of God."[38]

Many last-day events are held in suspension until this cleansing reaches that point where God will not be embarrassed to give His end-time people the promised latter rain.[39] The eyes of the unfallen universe are not on this world's dreary parade of wars, famines, and natural disasters as they try to figure out when Jesus will return. They have been patiently waiting for God's professed people to cooperate with Him in "hastening the advent" (2 Peter 3:12).[40]

- Now, our third "nuance" reflected in Daniel 8:14—"to vindicate."[41] God's loyalists in the end time eventually vindicate His patience, wisdom, and "grace to help in time of need" (Hebrews 4:16). In Ezekiel 36, we can see God's big picture as to how essential to His plan is the faithful response of His faithful people.

Running down parallel tracks in the end time, the truth about Satan and his wicked plans will be dramatically revealed as well as the truth about God's character and His promises to His faithful. In both cases, God is vindicated.[42]

I like the way Frank Holbrook put it:

> We must keep our reasoning straight here. The controversy which began with *God* does not merely end with the judgment of *man*. If it began with God, it must end with God. That is, if the great moral controversy which has troubled our universe for millennia began with false accusations against the Deity, it can only terminate—with a secure universe—if the Deity is cleared or vindicated of these charges. In actuality, God "cannot" reaffirm the justification of His genuine, repentant people unless He Himself and His plan of salvation are acknowledged by the loyal universe as true and just, and the same loyal intelligences agree with God that Satan is a wicked rebel and his accusations against God are false. The ultimate purpose of final judgment is not simply to vindicate an omniscient Deity, but also to draw all created intelligences both loyal and redeemed—and the lost—into a willing agreement with God and His view of matters.[43]

After outlining all this good news about the investigative judgment which God and His loyalists have looked forward to for thousands of years, one more thought needs to be said: For those living during this time of judgment, it should be their hour of rejoicing, not fear. Fear, yes, for those who have a wrong picture of God that Satan has painted so effectively since his rebellion in heaven. But for those who see God through Jesus, judgment time is good news—His coming is near!

Loyalists today rejoice in Daniel's categorical declaration that the investigative judgment is " 'made in favor of the saints of the Most High' " (Daniel 7:22). Loyalists rest in our Lord's assurance that " 'he who hears My word and believes in Him who sent Me has everlasting life, and shall not come into judgment, but has passed from death into life' " (John 5:24).

Loyalists sing with Job, even during tough times: " 'For I know that my Redeemer lives, And He shall stand at last on the earth; And after my skin is destroyed, this I know, That in my flesh I shall see God' " (Job 19:25, 26).

Loyalists daily thank the Lord for the assurance that they are "accepted in the Beloved" (Ephesians 1:6), that if they keep "walk[ing] in the light as He is in the light . . . the blood of Jesus Christ . . . cleanses us from all sin" (1 John 1:9), that all who make Jesus the Savior and Lord of their lives can claim His promise, " 'I give them eternal life and they shall never perish; neither shall anyone snatch them out of My hand. My Father who has given them to Me, is greater than all; and no one is able to snatch them out of My Father's hand' " (John 10:28, 29).

Loyalists have discovered that "the faith of Jesus" (Revelation 14:12) helps them to endure life's troubles, that "perfect love casts out fear" (1 John 4:18).

Men and women of faith are not afraid of the investigative judgment. They know that Jesus as their Intercessor, their Mediator, met Satan face to face on this earth. With the same human equipment we all have, without any special advantages, He proved that men and women this side of Eden can overcome any temptation hurled by Satan.[44] He gave us courage and took away our excuses. He not only led the way through a world of "fiery darts of the wicked one" (Ephesians 6:16) to show it could be done, He comes back through His Holy Spirit to give us the same power He had.[45] That is why John could pass on to us our Lord's promise that we too "may overcome" even as He "overcame" (Revelation 3:21).

In the investigative judgment, as our "all-powerful Mediator,"[46] Jesus can face down all of Satan's charges against His people. When Satan objects to God's rulings in favor of those men and women of faith who have honored Him with their loyalty, Jesus points first to His own unsullied record in His dueling with Satan; then He points to the records of His loyal followers, to their "diligent" faithfulness and their maturing faith trajectory.[47]

Further, His loyalists know that Jesus stands in the courts above as their High Priest today, not only as their Example showing the way to overcome sin, but also as their Enabler to help them prove

Satan wrong, even as He did. This insight sparkles with heavenly dynamics:

> Everyone who will break from the slavery and service of
> Satan, and will stand under the blood-stained banner of Prince
> Immanuel will be kept by Christ's intercessions. Christ, as our
> Mediator, at the right hand of the Father, ever keeps us in
> view, for it is as necessary that He should keep us by His inter-
> cessions as that He should redeem us with His blood. If He
> lets go His hold of us for one moment, Satan stands ready to
> destroy. Those purchased by His blood, He now keeps by His
> intercession.[48]

If I should see a man with a baseball bat entering the room behind
your back, my instincts would be to intercede and do all I could to
keep him from hurting you. I would be your "intercessor" at that
point in your life. Jesus is doing just that every hour of the day and
night for you through angels and the Holy Spirit.[49] We can count on
His powerful intercessions in our lives today, even as we have been count-
ing on the fact that He died for us on that horrible cross!

All that adds up to sky-high assurance for loyalists during the investigative judgment! One day soon, if we keep abiding in Christ, walking in the light He gives us daily, we will be part of that great multitude
that declares God's judgments to be "true and righteous" (Revelation
19:2). We will be part of the eternal answer to Satan's lies. We will be
part of the reason that guarantees to the unfallen worlds and unfallen
angels that the whole universe will finally and eternally be secure from
all rebellion.[50]

The faithful know that their loyalty to God is not based on their
efforts to seek His favor but in the sense of privilege that they can
honor God in "the hour of His judgment." The question always is: Do
I enjoy known duty, and am I responding as one who wants to honor
God in every aspect of my life? If so, God is winning, and Satan is
losing!

Those who live daily with the "assurance of faith" (Hebrews 10:22)
know, with a quiet humility, void of pride, that the investigative judgment is nothing more than an on-going record that reflects one's
daily walk with the Spirit. This heavenly review mirrors those in the
end time who have taken Peter's counsel seriously: "Therefore, since
all these things will be dissolved, what manner of persons ought you
to be in holy conduct and godliness, looking for and hastening the
coming of the day of God, because of which the heavens will be

dissolved being on fire, and the elements will melt with fervent heat" (2 Peter 3:11, 12).

I know the thought lingers: What happens if I lose this sense of God's leading in my life? Where do I stand when I really mess up my life, after I have had the rich assurance of a saving relationship with Jesus? What then?

Let's let the Lord and His apostles answer those questions. There is no despair in the "good news"!

---

[1] See pp. 11.

[2] See footnote 9 below. "The grace of God must be received by the sinner before he can be fitted for the kingdom of God. . . . As the leaven when mingled with the meal, works from within outward, so it is by the renewing of the heart that the grace of God works to transform the life" (Ellen G. White, *Christ's Object Lessons*, p. 97).

[3] See pp. 12.

[4] "Christ on the Mount of Olives pictured to His disciples the scene of the great judgment day. And He represented its decision as turning upon one point. When the nations are gathered before Him, there will be but two classes, and their eternal destiny will be determined by what they have done or have neglected to do for Him in the person of the poor and the suffering. *In that day Christ does not present before men the great work He has done for them in giving His life for their redemption. He presents the faithful work they have done for Him*" (Ellen G. White, *The Desire of Ages*, p. 637, italics supplied).

[5] "Those who refuse to cooperate with God on earth would not cooperate with Him in heaven. It would not be safe to take them to heaven" (Ellen G. White, *Christ's Object Lessons*, p. 280).

[6] "In the book of God's remembrance every deed of righteousness is immortalized. There every temptation resisted, every evil overcome, every word of tender pity expressed, is faithfully chronicled. And every act of sacrifice, every suffering and sorrow endured for Christ's sake, is recorded. . . . There is a record also of the sins of men. . . . The secret purposes and motives appear in the unerring register; for God 'will bring to light the hidden things of darkness, and will make manifest the counsels of the hearts.' 1 Corinthians 4:5. . . . Every man's work passes in review before God and is registered for faithfulness or unfaithfulness. Opposite each name in the books of heaven is entered with terrible exactness every wrong word, every selfish act, every unfulfilled duty, and every secret sin, with every artful dissembling. Heaven-sent warnings or reproofs neglected, wasted moments, unimproved opportunities, the influence exerted for good or for evil, with its far-reaching results, all are chronicled by the recording angel" (Ellen G. White, *The Great Controversy*, pp. 481,482).

[7] See footnote 9 below.

[8] Ellen G. White, *Steps to Christ*, pp. 57, 58.

[9] Ellen G. White, *Christ's Object Lessons*, pp. 315, 317, 319.

[10] Ellen G. White, *The Great Controversy*, p. 488.

[11] Ibid.

[12] Ibid.

[13] Ibid.

[14] Ellen G. White, *The Great Controversy*, p. 489.

[15] *Eternity*, September, 1965.

[16] "The intercession of Christ in man's behalf in the sanctuary above is as essential to the plan of salvation as was His death upon the cross. By His death He began that work which after His resurrection He ascended to complete in heaven" (Ellen G. White, *The Great Controversy*, p. 489).

[17] See Roy Gane, *Altar Call* (Berrien Springs, Mich.: Diadem, 1999); Frank Holbrook, *The Atoning Priesthood of Jesus Christ* (Berrien Springs, Mich.: Adventist Theological Society Publications, 1996); Arnold V. Wallenkampf, Richard Lesher, Frank B. Holbrook, editors, *The Sanctuary and the Atonement* (Silver Spring, Md.: Biblical Research Institute, 1989).

[18] See 1 Thessalonians 4:14-17. Might there be a connection between the investigative judgment and Paul's insight in 1 Corinthians 4:9—"For we have been made a spectacle to the world, both to angels and to men"?

[19] *The Great Controversy*, p. 425.

[20] 1 Corinthians 4:9—"spectacle [Literally, "theater"] to the world, both to angels and to men." That this planet is a stage for the universe to observe the interplay of good and evil and how every person since Adam has had his or her part to play in the drama, is an awesome thought. Imagine: "The Monarch of the universe and the myriads of heavenly angels are spectators . . . they are anxiously watching to see who will be successful overcomers, and win the crown of glory that fadeth not away" (Ellen G. White, *Testimonies for the Church*, vol. 4, p. 34). "The whole universe is looking with inexpressible interest to see the closing work of the great controversy between Christ and Satan. At such a time as this, just as the great work of judging the living is to begin, shall we allow unsanctified ambition to take possession of the heart?" (Ellen G. White, *Testimonies for the Church*, vol. 5, p. 526).

[21] *God in the Dock* (Grand Rapids, MI: William B. Eerdmans Publishing Company, 1970), p. 244.

[22] "The coming of Christ here described is not His second coming to the earth. He comes to the Ancient of Days in heaven to receive dominion, and glory, and a kingdom, which will be given Him at the close of His work as a mediator" (Ellen G. White, *The Great Controversy*, p. 480).

[23] For the validity of October 22, 1844, see Siegfried Horn and Lynn Wood, *The Chronology of Ezra 7*, 2nd Edition (Washington, D.C.: Review and Herald, 1970); William H. Shea, *Selected Studies on Prophetic Interpretation* (Washington, D.C.: Review and Herald, 1982), pp. 132, 137; William H. Shea, "When Did the Seventy Weeks of Daniel 9:24 Begin?" *Journal of the Adventist Theological Society*, vol. 2, no. 1, 1991.

[24] Ellen G. White, *The Great Controversy*, p. 480.

[25] See pp. 16–19.

[26] I think of John Greenleaf Whittier's lines in "Maud Muller"—"For of all sad words of tongue or pen, The saddest are these: 'It might have been!' "

[27] See previous chapter on "What Do Habits Have To Do With Assurance?"

[28] Richard M. Davidson, "In Confirmation of the Sanctuary Message," *Journal of the Adventist Theological Society*, vol. 2, no. 1, 1991; "The Meaning of Nitsdaq in Daniel 8:14," Ibid., vol. 7, no. 1, 1996.

[29] RSV (1952) reflects this understanding: ". . . then the sanctuary shall be restored to its rightful state"; TEV: ". . . will be restored."

[30] See Revelation 2:7, 11, 17, 26; 3:5, 12, 31.

[31] Dietrich Bonhoeffer's famous phrase.

[32] KJV, ASV, Moulton's.

[33] "In the ancient sanctuary the solemn services of the annual Day of Atonement brought the yearly ritual cycle to a close (Lev.16). The work of atonement, or reconciliation, performed on that day brought to completion all that the sanctuary and the priests could do for repentant sinners, and cleansed the sanctuary and the people" (Don F. Neufeld, editor, *The Seventh-day Adventist Encyclopedia,* Revised Edition [Washington, D.C.: Review and Herald, 1976], p. 95).

[34] Ellen G. White, *Education,* p. 36.

[35] Ibid.

[36] *Signs of the Times,* February 14, 1900.

[37] "By revealing in our own life the character of Christ we cooperate with Him in the work of saving souls. It is only by revealing in our life His character that we can co-operate with Him. And the wider the sphere of our influence, the more good we may do. When those who profess to serve God follow Christ's example, practicing the principles of the law in their daily life; when every act bears witness that they love God supremely and their neighbor as themselves, then will the church have power to move the world" (*Christ's Object Lessons,* p. 340).

[38] Cited in A. V. Olson, *Thirteen Crisis Years,* (Washington, D.C.: RHPA, 1981), p. 276.

[39] See Ellen G. White, *Testimonies for the Church,* vol. 5, p. 214.

[40] See Herbert E. Douglass, *The End* (Brushton, N.Y.: TEACH Services, Inc., 2001; PPPA, 1979), for thirty-one references in the writings of Ellen G. White which support Peter's admonition in 2 Peter 3:12.

[41] See NASB, margin. See *The International Critical Commentary* New York: Scribner's, 1927), p. 342. "A significant feature of the final judgment is the vindication of God's character before all the intelligences of the universe. The false charges that Satan has lodged against the government of God must be demonstrated as utterly groundless. God must be shown to have been entirely fair in the selection of certain individuals to make up His future kingdom, and in the barring of others from entrance there. . . . Thus the Heb. *sadaq* [cleansed, restore, vindicate] may convey the additional thought that God's character will be fully vindicated as the climax to 'the hour of his judgment' (Rev. 14:7), which began in 1844" (*SDABC,* vol. 4, p. 845).

[42] "In the antitype also, against Satan's false claim that God cannot fulfill His new covenant promises, God gathers an entire generation to Himself at the consummation of history who demonstrate the ultimate effectiveness of the gospel. . . . Not only do the *saints* serve to vindicate God's character. Ezekiel uses the same language to describe the final judgment upon the *wicked,* and in particular their leader (Ezekiel 38:16, 22, 23, RSV). The final judgment reveals not only the ultimate effectiveness of the gospel but also the full ripening of iniquity" (Richard M. Davidson, "The Good News of Yom Kippur," *Journal of the Adventist Theological Society,* vol. 2, no. 2, 1991).

[43] Frank B. Holbrook, *The Atoning Priesthood of Jesus Christ* (Berrien Springs, Mich.: Adventist Theological Society Publications, 1996), p. 174.

[44] See Ellen G. White, *The Desire of Ages,* pp. 24, 762,

[45] "The Spirit was to be given as a regenerating agent, and without this the sacrifice of Christ would have been of no avail. The power of evil had been strengthening for centuries, and the submission of men to this satanic captivity was amazing. Sin could be resisted and overcome only through the mighty agency of the Third Person of the Godhead, who would come with no modified energy, but in the fullness of divine power. It is the Spirit that makes effectual what has been wrought out by the world's Redeemer. It is by the Spirit that the heart is made pure. Through the Spirit

the believer becomes a partaker of the divine nature. Christ has given His Spirit as a divine power to overcome all hereditary and cultivated tendencies to evil, and to impress His own character upon His church" (Ibid., p. 671). "The Holy Spirit was promised to be with those who were wrestling for victory, in demonstration of all mightiness, endowing the human agent with supernatural powers, and instructing the ignorant in the mysteries of the kingdom of God. That the Holy Spirit is to be the grand helper, is a wonderful promise. Of what avail would it have been to us that the only begotten Son of God had humbled Himself, endured the temptations of the wily foe, and wrestled with him during His entire life on earth, and died the Just for the unjust, that humanity might not perish, if the Spirit had not been given as a constant, working, regenerating agent to make effectual in our cases what had been wrought out by the world's Redeemer" (*Manuscript Releases*, vol. 2, p. 14).

[46] Ellen G. White, *The Great Controversy*, p. 488.

[47] Ibid., p. 425.

[48] Ellen White Comments on Romans 8:34, *SDABC*, vol. 6, p. 1078.

[49] "The intercession of Christ in man's behalf in the sanctuary above is as essential to the plan of salvation as was His death upon the cross. By His death He began that work which after His resurrection He ascended to complete in heaven. We must by faith enter within the veil, 'whither the forerunner is for us entered.' Hebrews 6:20. There the light from the cross of Calvary is reflected. There we may gain a clearer insight into the mysteries of redemption. The salvation of man is accomplished at an infinite expense to heaven; the sacrifice made is equal to the broadest demands of the broken law of God. Jesus has opened the way to the Father's throne, and through His mediation the sincere desire of all who come to Him in faith may be presented before God" (Ellen G. White, *The Great Controversy*, p. 489).

[50] Ellen G. White, *The Desire of Ages*, p. 759.

CHAPTER SIXTEEN

Can Assurance Be Lost?

Sad even to think about it! But assurance can be lost—by neglect or by sheer stubbornness in wanting the pleasures of this world. Or by choosing the false assurances of a limited gospel that promises salvation without obedience and without character transformation.

Here again Christians must be realists. Paul knew from his own experience in working with his young churches that once-converted men and women can fall away and lose their saving relationship with Jesus.

Think of Demas, one of Paul's early supporters who left him. The record says that Demas "loved this present world" (Colossians 4:14; see also Philemon 24; 2 Timothy 4:10). Think of Hymenaeus (1 Timothy 1:20; 2 Timothy 2:17). He once had "faith and a good conscience" but rejected it, making "shipwreck" of his faith. He is remembered today for being among the first in the Christian church to sink into religious chatter and doctrinal subversion.

Demas and Hymenaeus both started out well. But love of this world and the false hope of an easier gospel led them away from their original church fellowship, to be remembered only with pity. How much damage they did to the church's witness is not known, but Paul's warnings would indicate that it may have been serious.

Paul had no allusions about the possibility that he himself could fall away (apostatize). The evil one surely had Paul in his cross-hairs. Probably no one in the early church had more temptations to call it quits. Paul not only knew the fury of his once-Jewish friends in high circles, he felt the sting of his own church members ("perils among false brethren"—2 Corinthians 11:26). He had to contend with church leadership who needed to learn from him what the full gospel was (see Acts 15). In other words, he had to go it alone, so much like our Savior!

So, reality led Paul to share with others his own daily focus: "I discipline my body and bring it into subjection, lest, when I have preached to others, I myself should become disqualified" (1 Corinthians 9:27). Can anyone waltz around that lucid fact that even the best of Christian leaders could lose his saving relationship with Jesus?

Paul saw another way that fellow Christians could lose a genuine sense of assurance. In Romans, he appealed to those who wandered into a presumptuous assurance wherein their "faith" was a substitute for obedience (see Romans 6). In Galatians, Paul was concerned with a presumptuous assurance from the other direction, wherein their "faith" was resting on their misunderstanding of the Jewish rituals and the purpose of law in general. "You have become estranged from Christ, you who attempt to be justified by law, you have fallen from grace" (Galatians 5:4). We see these two groups thriving in the Christian church today—neither one truly understanding either the everlasting covenant or the everlasting gospel.

In the book of Hebrews, we have clear warnings given to those who once experienced the joy of salvation. Paul wanted his hearers to learn the lesson of the Israelites, God's chosen people. The Israelites are a standing example of those who once enjoyed dramatic evidence that God was leading them individually and as a nation. Their affirmations, on many occasions, witnessed to the world the sense of a saving relationship with their God.

But too often genuine assurance went downhill to presumptuous assurance. Note Paul's warning: "Beware brethren, lest there be in any of you an evil heart of unbelief [Greek: "unfaith"] in departing from the living God" (Hebrews 3:12). Their problem was not that they no longer believed in the facts of the Exodus or in the facts regarding the sanctuary service (that is, their problem was not that of "belief"); their problem was "faith"—they did not continue to let God be their Ruler as well as their Savior. For them, this faith relationship with God turned into an external behavioral system to the extent that the prophet Micah had to say:

> With what shall I come before the Lord,
> And bow myself before the High God?
> Shall I come before Him with burnt offerings,
> With calves a year old?

Will the Lord be pleased with thousands of rams
Or ten thousand rivers of oil?
Shall I give my firstborn for my transgression,
The fruit of my body for the sin of my soul?

He has shown you, O man, what is good;
And what does the Lord require of you
But to do justly,
To love mercy,
And to walk humbly with your God? (6:6-8).

In the sixth chapter of Hebrews Paul gives another warning of a different kind which at first glance seems to shut the door on anyone who wants to return to Christian fellowship after open sin. Let's look at those words which have caused much discouragement for backslidden Christians who want to repent:

> For it is impossible for those who were once enlightened, and have tasted the heavenly gift, and have become partakers of the Holy Spirit, and have tasted the good word of God and the powers of the age to come, if they fall away, to renew them again in repentance, since they crucify again for themselves the Son of God, and put Him to an open shame (verses 4-6).

The Greek construction permits the following points;

- The context implies that repentance is impossible for a person who has *no desire* to return to a saving relationship with Jesus.
- Repentance is impossible while one *keeps on crucifying* the Son of God—that is, while the person is unrepentant.
- Repentance is impossible for one who *keeps on holding up Christ to contempt.*

In other words, Paul is sounding a clear and present danger to all Christians that slipping into sinful practices, turning from any light that the Spirit has given, they could ultimately cross that line when conscience no longer accuses, when no remorse for sinful practices exists.

Paul is not saying that a backsliding Christian has gone too far if he or she has an awakened conscience and is truly sorry for sinful practices. If anyone has a sincere desire to return to a saving relationship with Jesus, that, in itself, is a sign that the unpardonable sin has not been committed. To the contrary, such remorse is a sign that Jesus is speaking directly to him or her. " 'I have this against you, that you have left your first love. Remember therefore from where you have fallen; repent and do the first works' " (Revelation 2:4, 5).

Isn't that good news? It breathes our Lord's enduring promise: " 'The one who comes to Me I will by no means cast out' " (John 6:37). *Only sinners who refuse to return to their heavenly Father, who refuse to respond to the voice of the Holy Spirit, can shut the door of mercy, not Jesus or the Holy Spirit.*

In Hebrews 10, Paul gave a similar message warning of the clear and present danger to those who dally with sin:

> Let us hold fast the confession of our hope, without wavering, for He who promised is faithful. . . . For if we [continue to] sin willfully after we have received the [full, experiential] knowledge of the truth, there no longer remains a sacrifice for sins, but a certain fearful expectation of judgment, and fiery indignation which will devour the adversaries. Anyone who has rejected Moses' law dies without mercy on the testimony of two or three witnesses. Of how much worse punishment, do you suppose, will he be thought worthy who has trampled the Son of God underfoot, counted the blood of the covenant by which he was sanctified a common thing, and insulted the Spirit of grace (verses 23, 26-29).

Could a warning be clearer? It gives me goose pimples! Again, the Greek construction will help us understand what Paul is saying:

- The person who *continues to sin* willfully, who *persistently renounces* his former vows to serve Jesus, will eventually cross the line and commit the unpardonable sin—the deliberate rejection of the Holy Spirit's appeals.
- The person who rejects the "full knowledge" of what it means to be a Christian is here described, not the person who has not yet fully grasped what a saving relationship to Jesus means.
- The person here described is *deliberately scoffing* at his former Christian commitment, openly ridiculing his Christian friends and their loyalty to their Lord, letting the world know that he despises his former relationship with Jesus.

Paul continued his "fatherly" appeal to early Christians who indeed faced tough decisions in a very unfriendly world:

Therefore do not cast away your confidence, which has great reward. For you have need of endurance, so that after you have done the will of God, you may receive the promise: "For yet a little while, and he who is coming will come and will not tarry. Now the just shall live by faith: But if anyone draws back, My soul has no pleasure in him." But we are not of those who draw back to perdition, but of those who believe [have faith] to the saving of the soul (10:35-39).

Sounds like counsel that should be heard often in our Sabbath sermons! Here again are very positive points that Paul is driving home with impressive logic:

- Christians are to hold fast to the truths that led them to a saving relationship with Jesus—some apparently are not "holding on."
- Christians are to develop the habit of endurance, a special characteristic of those described in Revelation 14:12: "Here is the patience [Greek: endurance] of the saints . . ."
- Christians are, by definition, committed to doing the will of God (Matthew 7:21-27).
- Faith, a genuine relationship with Jesus that includes a belief in His role as both Savior and Ruler, a trust in His keeping power, an appreciation for His magnificent, forever gift of Himself to humanity, and a heart-willingness to follow Him and His instructions wherever He leads—all this marks one who is cooperating with God in the "saving" of his or her soul.

Peter adds his voice to the clear and present danger about which Paul warned:

For if, after they have escaped the pollutions of the world through the [Greek: full, experiential] knowledge of the Lord and Savior Jesus Christ, they are again entangled in them and overcome, the latter end is worse for them than the beginning. For it would have been better for them not to have known the way of righteousness, than having known it to turn from the holy commandment delivered to them (2 Peter 2:20, 21).

You can hear the old fisherman talking—nothing academic about his letters! Peter is especially warning against religious leaders who were once spiritual leaders in the Christian church, but who have now left the church and are ambitious to lead others to follow them. "They have forsaken the right way and gone astray. . . . These are wells without water. . . . They promise them liberty, they themselves are slaves" (2 Peter 2:15-19).

Could any warning be more up-to-date—this description of former church leaders who, from the outside, promise their former church friends the "good news" that will liberate them from bondage to unnecessary restrictions?

What can Peter tell us about those who once had a saving relationship with Jesus?

- For Christians who once had an experiential knowledge of Jesus (a saving relationship that gave them genuine assurance), to forsake this experience, "the latter end is worse for them than the beginning" (2 Peter 2:20). Why? The Christian who goes back to his former world of various "pollutions" is forsaking a deeply rich experience that came with the new birth and early walk with Jesus. He had learned through experience (Greek: experiential knowledge) how powerful the Holy Spirit was in his life as he forsook his worldly habits. But now, going back to his former practices, his heart is hardened to appeals that pagans would respond to. He is no longer susceptible to the gospel as he once was.
- Peter is concerned that new church members should not be charmed and enticed by those who promise the gospel of liberty, substituting faith for obedience. Evil appeals can make "liberty" very attractive but liberty is often the door to self-indulgent pleasures. True liberty untangles the believer from self-destructive habits; Peter calls that liberty "the way of righteousness."
- Peter like Paul is concerned about former church members who *continue* in their "entanglements" and who have allowed themselves to become spiritually hardened to the appeals of the Holy Spirit.

Jude, the brother of James, echoed the clear and present warnings of both Paul and Peter:

> Beloved, while I was very diligent to write to you concerning our common salvation I found it necessary to write to you exhorting you to contend earnestly for the faith which was once for all delivered to the saints. For certain men have crept in unnoticed, who long ago were marked out for this condemnation, ungodly men, who turn the grace of our God into licentiousness. . . . But I want to remind you, though you once knew this, that the Lord, having saved the people out of the

land of Egypt, afterward destroyed those who did not believe [have faith] (Jude 3, 5).

- Again, these three apostles saw the attractive danger of former members who can fast-talk their own escape from obedience to the Lord into a new experience of liberty—"turning the grace of our God into licentiousness."
- Nothing has been more seductive throughout Christian history than the deception that God's grace somehow eliminates human responsibility. For some, grace somehow accepts and approves and saves men and women unconditionally, if they only have acknowledged that Jesus died for them. These want the liberty of knowing sins are forgiven, though they are not forsaken.
- The reason for all apostasy, for all drifting away from a saving relationship with Jesus, is the numbing of faith. Throughout this book we have been focusing on faith as the one factor that will determine a person's eternal future. Faith, the human response to grace, describes a trusting, joyfully complying, man or woman who will follow Jesus and His Word wherever they lead.

John continues these strong warnings as well as strong appeals for Christians to remain steadfast amidst the various temptations that could muddy their faith experience. Note how he gently but firmly unites bad news with good news:

"Nevertheless I have this against you, that you have left your first love. Remember therefore from where you have fallen; repent and do the first works, or else I will come to you quickly and remove your lampstand from its place—unless you repent" (Revelation 2:4, 5).

"Hold fast what you have till I come. And he who overcomes, and keeps My works until the end, to him I will give power over the nations" (Revelation 2:25, 26).

"Be watchful, and strengthen the things which remain, that are ready to die, for I have not found your works perfect before God. Remember therefore how you have received and heard; hold fast and repent. Therefore if you will not watch, I will come upon you as a thief, and you will not know what hour I will come upon you" (Revelation 3:2, 3).

"Hold fast what you have, that no one may take your crown.

He who overcomes I will make him a pillar in the temple of My God, and he shall go out no more. And I will write on him the name of My God" (Revelation 3:11, 12).

"Behold, I stand at the door and knock. If anyone hears My voice and opens the door, I will come in to him and dine with him, and he with Me. To him who overcomes I will grant to sit with Me on My throne, as I also overcame and sat down with My Father on His throne" (Revelation 3:20, 21).

These solemn words need no commentary. How can anyone add to the gravity of these invitations and warnings? The message is clear: Christians can fall from their assurance of salvation, and they can regain it by repenting—that is, confessing and forsaking known sin (see Proverbs 28:13; 1 John 1:9).

We all know from experience about cloudy days when we "are ready to doubt whether [our] hearts have been renewed by the Holy Spirit." To such Ellen White has said:

Do not draw back in despair. We shall often have to bow down and weep at the feet of Jesus because of our shortcomings and mistakes, but we are not to be discouraged. Even if we are overcome by the enemy, we are not cast off, not forsaken and rejected of God. No; Christ is at the right hand of God, who also maketh intercession for us. Said the beloved John, "These things write I unto you, that ye sin not. And if any man sin, we have an advocate with the Father, Jesus Christ the righteous." 1 John 2:1. And do not forget the words of Christ, "The Father Himself loveth you." John 16:27. He desires to restore you to Himself, to see His own purity and holiness reflected in you. And if you will but yield yourself to Him, He that hath begun a good work in you will carry it forward to the day of Jesus Christ. . . .

The closer you come to Jesus, the more faulty you will appear in your own eyes; for your vision will be clearer, and your imperfections will be seen in broad and distinct contrast to His perfect nature. This is evidence that Satan's delusions have lost their power; that the vivifying influence of the Spirit of God is arousing you.[1]

I think that everyone should have the above paragraph in *Steps to Christ* marked carefully and read it often!

It seems that the bottom line of this chapter is this:

- This side of the resurrection or the Advent, "we shall have self to subdue, besetting sins to overcome; so long as life shall last, there will be no stopping place, no point which we can reach and say, I have fully attained. Sanctification is the result of lifelong obedience."[2]
- And yet, with the genuine Christian's "consent, He [Jesus] will so identify Himself with our thoughts and aims, so blend our hearts and minds into conformity to His will, that when obeying Him we shall be but carrying out our own impulses. . . . When we know God as it is our privilege to know Him, our life will be a life of continual obedience. Through an appreciation of the character of Christ, through communion with God, sin will become hateful to us."[3]

I like that phrase that we have been emphasizing often through these pages—that we can never reach the place in Christian growth when we can say that we have "fully attained." That sounds just like God! He has so much in mind for us that after two billion years in eternity, we still will be very aware that we have not "fully attained." Read again those promises in the last chapter!

I remember the day when I took my children to Saratoga, New York. In 1777, the second battle of Saratoga of the American Revolution gave the young Continental army one of its most decisive victories. I wanted my children to see a very interesting monument in the cemetery near the battlefield. The monument is dedicated to four generals of the American Continental army who were in command of their groups during that remarkable colonial victory.

General Gates was supreme commander that day, chiefly, they say, because of his political skill rather than his military merit. The battle for Saratoga would have been lost if Gates had not received the dashing heroism of Benedict Arnold at the right time. Reports say that Benedict Arnold late in the day did more with his 3,000 men than Gates did all day with his 11,000. Benedict Arnold was second only to Washington in the eyes of the Continental soldier.

But that monument! On that four-sided obelisk today you will find the name and statue of Generals Gates, Schuyler, and Morgan. But on the fourth side, an empty niche remains for the hero of Saratoga. We pondered what could have been!

However, I especially wanted my children to see a second monument on the battlefield itself. Much, much smaller than the obelisk is a statue of a boot, the boot of Benedict Arnold. In the evening of the battle of Saratoga, a wounded Hessian soldier, lying on the ground, fired at Arnold, shattering his left leg, the same leg that had been wounded in Quebec. A rifleman, rushed upon the Hessian with drawn bayonet. He was stopped only by Arnold's cry: "For God's sake, don't hurt him!" It has been well said that that was the hour when the brilliant young general should have died.

A few months later, General Benedict Arnold, the commander of the fort at West Point, was plotting to turn the fort over to the British! By a chance coincidence, he was discovered, and he fled for his life to the British. The profit he received for his treason was a few thousand dollars and a commission in the British Army.

After becoming a Britisher, he asked an American prisoner, "What would the Americans do if they caught me?" With contempt the American said: "They would cut off your wounded leg and give it the best of military burials—then, they would hang the rest of you."

So today there is an empty niche in the monument at Saratoga, New York. Benedict Arnold started well, but he didn't end well. Have you ever heard of a child named Benedict or Judas or Adolf? Everybody leaves some mark when they die. Happy memories for children to treasure, great legacies of worthy books or mighty industries. Or prison records or disappointed children or a boot! How will you be remembered?

Jesus has given us all a sober warning: " 'He who endures to the end will be saved' " (Matthew 10:22).

One of these days there will be a long table set with the best of Rodgers silver and better than Blue Willow or Wedgewood china. In some way, a name card will be at each plate because everyone has been invited. You can be sure that there will be fathers and mothers going up and down that long table looking for a son or daughter. Or children looking for their parents. Or a wife looking for her husband, a husband looking for his mate. Or sweethearts separated by war.

But, there will be empty seats at that table—just like Benedict Arnold's name was missing from the monument. Many of those missing ones started out well, but for the many reasons we have discussed in these pages, they changed leaders in their spiritual journeys. Many of them redefined "faith" and substituted it for obedience to their Lord. Others drifted into the current of least resistance, enjoying immediate gratifications. Whatever the reason, trading eternity for a few "fun" years on this earth is a poor bargain.

The last word will be sung by that mighty choir, " 'Alleluia! Salvation and glory and honor and power to the Lord our God! For true and righteous are His judgments' " (Revelation 19:1, 2)! Will you be in your place, singing out what you have found to be true—that God has been super faithful, that He can be trusted, and that you will serve Him forever?

The greatest calamity would be parents looking in vain for their children, children who did not put the "Son of God . . . to an open shame" (Hebrews 6:6), but who drifted for years without the joy of assurance, who in the end closed their life in despair as they questioned the reality of salvation. All that need not to have been!

Let us make Paul's appeal our personal life text: "Having a High Priest over the house of God, let us draw near with a true heart in full assurance of faith, having our hearts sprinkled from an evil conscience and our bodies washed with pure water. Let us hold fast the confession of our hope without wavering, for He who promised is faithful" (Hebrews 10:21-23).

The last word is not our faithfulness, but the faithfulness of God who has promised!

But what if all these reasonable and logical admonitions seem like too much burden? Is there any hope for the "losers" who have often given their hearts to Jesus only to fall under the burden of responsibility? Can we summarize the "good news" in a way that many have not seen it before? In our last chapter, let's sum up the "good news" which always gets better.

---

[1] *Steps to Christ*, pp. 64, 65.
[2] Ellen G. White, *The Acts of the Apostles*, pp. 560, 561.
[3] Ellen G. White, *The Desire of Ages*, p. 668.

17

The Good News Always Gets Better

Looking back over these pages, some readers may still think that "being saved" and experiencing "genuine assurance" puts more responsibility on them than they can carry. All that they have read here may sound very logical and encouraging but they have experienced too many failures to try again!

For some, trying and failing over and over again sets up a dark cloud that eclipses hope. They know all these principles do work for many around them. They see the difference in others, but they are convinced that whatever they try will soon end in failure. They have a record of failure.

Even though responsibility is reasonable and logical, to hear it after so many failures sends them into a spiritual tailspin. They understand the words, but not the music! They see only stern duty without the joy of salvation.

I have watched this scenario repeated over and over again for more than fifty years. I have reached out to these dear people with encouragement and hope. But until I clearly and firmly saw and experienced the principles set forth in this book, my best efforts were often not good enough.

Let's review these principles before we close. Jesus wants us to remember that:

- We are to trust God's faithfulness rather than our faithfulness (see Mark 11:22).[1]
- Our salvation depends not primarily on our diligence in making

good choices, but on God who works in us "both to will and to do of His good pleasure" (Philippians 2:13).

- God "who began this good work in you, will carry it on until it is finished on the Day of Jesus Christ" (Philippians 1:6, Good News Bible).
- God was looking for us before we thought of Him. He is the seeking Shepherd, and we all are His lost sheep (see Luke 15). The sheep rejoices that it is found, not in its determination to get God's attention. He is looking for you every morning before you awaken!
- He died for everyone of us! Our appreciation leads us to confession of failure and sinfulness then to repentance—not the other way around.[2]
- "God has made provision that we may become like unto Him, and He will accomplish this for all who do not interpose a perverse will and thus frustrate His grace."[3] Further, let's get this straight no matter what others tell us: "Do not conclude that the upward path is the hard and the downward road the easy way. . . . God's love has made it hard for the heedless and headstrong to destroy themselves."[4] And further, listen to this promise: "The sinner may resist this love, may refuse to be drawn to Christ; but if he does not resist, he will be drawn to Jesus; a knowledge of the plan of salvation will lead him to the foot of the cross in repentance for his sins, which have caused the sufferings of God's dear Son."[5] Bottom line: No one is lost because he or she is a sinner; we are lost because we frustrate God's grace and turn from the light (see John 3:17-21).[6]
- We can trust the Hand that was nailed to the cross. He wants us to know that He is always by our side through His Holy Spirit to prompt us when we are distracted, to empower us when our ACH is high and our GABA is low.[7]
- God is not waiting for us to maintain a saving relationship with Him; He wants us to know that He is maintaining that relationship with us!
- God's love for sinners is greater than His hatred for sin. "While God's hatred of sin is as strong as death, His love for the sinner is stronger than death. Having undertaken our redemption, He will spare nothing, however dear, which is necessary to the completion of His work. No truth essential to our salvation is withheld, no miracle of mercy is neglected, no divine agency is left unemployed. Favor is heaped upon favor, gift upon gift. The whole treasury of heaven is open to those He seeks to save. Having collected the

riches of the universe, and laid open the resources of infinite power, He gives them all into the hands of Christ, and says, All these are for man. Use these gifts to convince him that there is no love greater than Mine in earth or heaven. His greatest happiness will be found in loving Me."[8]

- All the biblical knowledge we may have in our heads will not give us the joy of genuine assurance. Genuine assurance is grounded on the simple formula: We give all to Christ in absolute surrender and self-denial, and we take all from Christ—all the right responses to temptation, to serving others, to improving our usefulness to serve, etc., that He will live out in our lives.

- The grace of God seeks us out, no matter where we may be and no matter how messy our lives may be—but God never leaves us where He finds us. What a future He has for each of us!

I remember a speaking appointment in Corpus Christi, Texas, a few months ago. During some free time, Norma and I visited the USS *Lexington*. It is the fifth ship in U.S. history to have that heroic name. The fourth was lost in the Battle of the Coral Sea (May 1942) after a brilliant and brave effort that stopped the advance of the Japanese toward Australia. As soon as this news hit America, the next aircraft carrier being built was named the *Lexington*, which also soon saw gallant action in the Pacific.

On December 4, 1943, this new *Lexington* was disabled by a Japanese bomber on a moonlit night off Tarawa. The skipper, Captain Felix Stump went to the ship's speaker system so that all aboard could hear him: "This is the captain speaking. We have taken a torpedo hit in our stern, and the rudder seems badly damaged. *Each man must do his job calmly and efficiently. Don't worry. That's my job. I got you here, and I'll get you out and home.*" And so he did. How he did it is a marvelous story.

But there's more to that story. More than 95 percent of those on board had never been in the open sea before. They were not seasoned sailors and pilots; they were citizen sailors and pilots—recently assembled; trained, but unsure of themselves. On that moonlit night, they were an easy target, but the captain kept maneuvering the ship into the moonlight so that the *Lexington* would not give the bomber or submarine a broadside silhouette. All the time changing his speed and direction.

On their way back to Pearl Harbor with that disabled rudder, the admiral of the fleet radioed to Captain Stump, "That was wonderful seamanship, Captain." The captain replied, *"Thank you, sir; my crew was magnificent!"*

Those words swept through the crew. They were magnificent in the eyes of their captain! The sailors wrote home about their captain. When they limped back to Pearl Harbor, they didn't need the serenade of the Navy Band to make them feel like they were heroes. They had already heard the commendation of their captain. Knowing their captain for what he was kept them unafraid, kept them doing their duty. They could trust their captain, because he got them there, and he would get them home.

One of these days, a wonderful group of people will, in a way, limp into the harbor after the worst time of trouble ever to hit people on this earth. And they will hear their Captain say, " ' "Well done, good and faithful servant. . . . Enter into the joy of your lord" ' " (Matthew 25:21).

And then He will turn to the unfallen worlds, to the unfallen angels, and wave His hand over the veterans from earth, and say, "My crew was magnificent!"

---

[1] A literal translation: "Keep holding on to God's faithfulness."

[2] The Greek word for "repentance" carries the meaning that the mind is changed, that a new life away from sin and failure is the sinner's daily choice.

[3] Ellen G. White, *God's Amazing Grace*, p. 134.

[4] Ellen G. White, *Thoughts From the Mount of Blessing*, p. 139. "The sinner may resist this love, may refuse to be drawn to Christ; but if he does not resist, he will be drawn to Jesus; a knowledge of the plan of salvation will lead him to the foot of the cross in repentance for his sins, which have caused the sufferings of God's dear Son" (*Steps to Christ*, p. 27; see also *The Desire of Ages*, p. 176). "Unless His followers choose to leave Him, He will hold them fast" (*The Desire of Ages*, p. 483).

[5] Ellen G. White, *Steps to Christ*, p. 27.

[6] Ellen G. White, *God's Amazing Grace*, p. 134.

[7] See pp. 118–125.

[8] Ellen G. White, *The Desire of Ages*, p. 57.

If you enjoyed this book, you'll enjoy these as well:

Why Jesus Waits
Herbert E. Douglass. A classic explanation about Jesus as the heart of the sanctuary service, and the empowerment from Him that enables ordinary Christians to live a life like His.
0-8163-1857-3. Paperback.
US$8.99, Can$14.49.

By His Stripes
Clifford Goldstein. A passionate, sometimes shocking, reexamination of the great controversy and the glory of redemption through the gospel of Isaiah—a book that has more to say about God's love, creation, free will, salvation, justice, and righteousness—than almost any other book of the Bible. 0-8163-1699-6. Hardcover.
US$10.97, Can$17.97.

Saving Blood
Keavin Hayden and *David Merrill.* A compelling new look at how Jesus saves us and why He is the center of our hope. In this analysis of how grace works, readers will find comfort, new courage for the battle, and a deeper appreciation of God's relentless love.
0-8163-1767-4. Paperback.
US$6.97, Can$11.47.

Order from your ABC by calling **1-800-765-6955**, or get online and shop our virtual store at **www.AdventistBookCenter.com**.
- Read a chapter from your favorite book
- Order online
- Sign up for email notices on new products